Problem Solving and Communication

Career Paths Vol. 5: Master All Challenges That Confront You

James Bellerjeau

A Fine Idea

Contents

Introduction

G reetings readers and congratulations! Simply by virtue of being here, you are already on the path to increasing your odds of success.

Our focus is on how to solve the many problems we'll be confronted with in our lives. An optimist assumes they'll never face obstacles. A pessimist worries that they will never get past them. A pragmatist knows that obstacles are both inevitable and opportunities to shine.

We pair communication with problem-solving because poor communication will make most problems worse and good communication holds the key to solving many others. We'll confront head-on the inescapable truth that it is the lies we tell ourselves that represent some of the most harmful kinds of communication.

Drawing on hard won experience and the lessons of philosophers across time, we'll explore what allows the skilled problem-solver to overcome difficult situations and thrive.

Although I'll cover a lot of ground with these lessons, you should consider them foundational rather than comprehensive. There are additional approaches to overcoming obstacles and succeeding at work, which you will find in the companion volumes of the **Career Paths** series.

Be well.

Chapter One

Don't Mistake Certainty for Correctness

We can be just as wrong about something when we are convinced it's true as when we're uncertain

It is easy to see when someone else is being pigheaded. The most obvious sign is that they disagree with you.

The ones who particularly get our goat, though, are the ones who zealously defend their position against all reason. These people refuse to be swayed by all the facts and evidence that point to them being wrong.

Don't they see how their certainty just makes them foolish?

No matter how often we observe this in others, I find it fascinating that the fewest among us make the link to *how we are perceived* when we are certain about something ourselves.

After all, when we're certain it's because we're right. When other people are certain it's because they're idiots who don't know how to think.

Is it possible you are right all the time?

I suppose it's possible some people are true savants, making correct assessments of all situations all the time. Based on decades of careful observation, I'm guessing the number of such persons is small.

Sadly, the odds are good that you and I are not among the perfect savants.

For starters, anyone who has been married must readily concede that *no one is right all the time.* You need only consider all the times your spouse correctly pointed out you were wrong about something to know the truth of this.

And we can be just as wrong about something when we are convinced it's true as when we're uncertain.

I do need to add one small caveat for the women readers. Many men have learned the wisdom of the phrase "Happy wife, happy life." This generates in men a greatly increased propensity to use the phrase "You're right, dear."

Your spouse saying you are right does not necessarily mean that you are right in fact, although you probably are if I'm being honest. But that is a topic for another day.

What happens when we're certain we're correct

Being convinced we're right, however, carries with it several heavy burdens:

- We become closed to new inputs and tend to seek out evidence to confirm our existing beliefs (confirmation bias)

- We make worse decisions because we stop seeking out new or contradictory information

- To justify our bad decisions, we shift blame to other people and factors outside our control

I have had the good fortune of having my many errors happily pointed out to me by friends and family. And they've been doing it for years!

Interestingly, my conviction is still as strong as ever, no matter how many times I am proven mistaken. When we think we are right, we can't help but think we're right.

How to be passionately wrong less often

Knowing the dangers implicit in this facet of human nature, is there anything we can do?

In my case, the frequent reminders of my fallibility have brought me one very useful practice that I try to apply whenever I can: I leave open the possibility that I may be wrong.

I still believe what I believe is true, but I will now often add to the end of a statement the words "but I could be wrong." That phrase is almost magical in its import. It accomplishes many things.

When you add "... but I could be wrong" to the end of a statement:

1. It means in your mind you are not committed to the absolute truth of what you just said. As a result, you can listen to what others say.

2. It means the person you are talking with does not consider you closed and is more likely *to listen to you*. This creates the condition for a dialogue in which you are as interested in learning something as you are in making a point.

3. Because you are less emotionally committed to what you said, it means you are less likely to feel compelled to defend it against all attacks. If it is just something you are discussing and not a personally-held belief, an attack on the statement is not an attack on you.

If you like the idea that being certain is no guarantee of being correct, then you are already on the path to better decision-making.

If you further agree that small changes made consistently can create great results (continuous improvement), then perhaps you will try out saying "But I could be wrong" yourself.

Be well.

Chapter Two

If You Ask the Wrong Questions...

You likely have many unexamined ideas and beliefs about why things happen the way they do

Have you heard the proverb, "There are none so blind as those who will not see"? We've all experienced it, usually when arguing with some idiot who disagrees with us on a perfectly obvious point.

Today I will explain the psychological grounding behind the phenomenon and give you some tips for how to avoid selective blindness yourself.

If you want to become well-informed on a topic, conducting broad research is essential.

Looking at the first few links in a Google search will give you a certain set of information, true. This will likely be mainstream information, meaning that either Google is promoting it or it is consistent with the majority view, or both.

Either way, you will probably not be widely criticized for parroting what most people already believe or can find in a quick search.

Because we do not like feeling uncomfortable, our natural tendency is to seek out information that conforms to our existing beliefs and to ignore conflicting information.

There is a more pernicious problem in conducting research, which is this: We are our own worst enemies. Being confronted with information that conflicts with our existing beliefs makes us uncomfortable, a situation referred to as cognitive dissonance.

Because we do not like feeling uncomfortable, our natural tendency is to seek out information that conforms to our existing beliefs and to ignore conflicting information.

Wellbeing ≠ Being right all the time

One way to counteract this tendency is to leave open the possibility that we may be wrong. In other words, not to tie our psychological well-being to being right all the time.

I discuss ways to do this in the preceding chapter. Not needing to be right is a helpful, if modest step.

Now I hear some of you saying: "This doesn't apply to me, at least not all the time. When I am doing research, I don't usually have a preconceived idea of what the answer is. I can't be affected by cognitive bias."

Not so fast, my friends. You may not have thought deeply about the issue you are researching, but you nonetheless are likely to have ideas about it.

"What do you mean? How can that be?"

Our understanding of the world and how it works is a complex, multi-layered construct, built up over the whole of our experiences. Some beliefs are at the forefront of your consciousness, and so you think of them as your core beliefs or values.

But you likely have many unexamined ideas and beliefs about why things happen the way they do. Humans are amazing pattern-recognition machines, so much so that we regularly and easily see patterns where none exist, finding causality in random correlation.

Even when you approach a topic with what you think is an open mind, you are coming with a lifetime of experiences that have shaped not only what you believe, but the very process of how you form new opinions.

Even if you don't cling to the need to be right, it can hurt when your belief system does not match up with new evidence.

A far more powerful way to counteract your cognitive biases is to *actively seek out information* that conflicts with your current view.

You will not do this by accident. It requires deliberate effort. But that effort does not have to be burdensome.

Some of the smartest people I know view it as a game. They love finding contradictory information because it means they've learned something about the world or themselves.

In this light, discovering you were wrong about something can be a gift. Thinking about it that way is a fine way to remove the potential sting of cognitive dissonance.

Do you want an interim test of what I'm talking about?

Some of you may have noticed a little frisson of displeasure when I suggested above that Google promotes certain views (and thus, by definition, must suppress others).

Because that is inconsistent with what many of you think about Google, i.e., they're just a search algorithm and they don't put a thumb on the scale. You either dismissed it without realizing it or you didn't even notice I wrote it.

Okay, don't believe me. Check for yourself. I'll wait.

There is an alternative search engine called DuckDuckGo. Search for something in Google, and then do the same search in DuckDuckGo.

- See how much overlap there is, and whether you detect any skew in the results.

- It will be easier to see the effect if you use a more polarizing topic, say "Trump indictment."

Identify blind spots

To sum up: We are biased, pattern-recognition machines, predisposed to confirm what we already believe, even if we don't know we believe it.

By reminding ourselves that we are fallible, and making a game of trying to identify our blind spots, we can improve the chances that we are looking at the world with relatively clear eyes.

These steps will help ensure that we not only ask better questions but that the answers we get are useful to us.

Be well.

Chapter Three

A Conversation Is the Worst Way to Communicate

It seems to me that there are more people shouting at each other than ever before

I suggest that a conversation is the worst way to communicate, at least if you are personally taking part in it. Why should this be so, you ask?

For a person to learn new information, they need to be open to receiving it. In a conversation, this means actively listening to what the other person is saying and making a conscious effort to understand it.

In my experience, people rarely demonstrate such purposeful listening.

You may see active listening occur in some professional settings, where there is some formalism to the exchange. For example, in a mediation where one side talks and then the other side talks, or where there is a clear hierarchy with one person speaking first and then others responding.

Outside such formal exchanges, the typical conversation is fluid, fast-moving, and unstructured.

- As a participant, you are expending a significant portion of your mental processing power planning your response.

- You are thinking about what will you say when the other person finally stops blabbing and lets you get a word in edgewise.

In contrast, **listening** to a good conversation can be a pleasure. This is why interview podcasts of two people talking are so popular.

It is much easier to pay attention to what both sides are saying when you are not a participant in the conversation and when you do not have to think of a response. Plus, because you chose the podcast and are listening to it for pleasure, you are a willing participant.

Listen to understand

If you want to increase your chances of being heard by your conversational partner, try approaching your next conversation with only one goal: listening to the other person and understanding their point.

Make an effort to summarize and repeat back what you heard and ask your conversational partner if that is what they meant. You may be surprised by how much this increases their willingness and ability to listen to you.

And if you are not trying to talk over the other person, the conversation feels more like a true give-and-take and less like a shouting match.

In fairness, communication is difficult under the best of circumstances, regardless of the means used. You would think that it would be easier to communicate with people in written form.

"Surely if I write something down in a short, simple memo, everyone will understand what I mean, right?" Sorry, no.

Here's what really happens when you send out a memo:

- At least a third of your audience will not see or even bother to read what you have written.

- Another depressingly large portion will not take away what you intended. This is because people read and hear what they want to see, not what is objectively in front of them.

- Most of the minority that read your memo and understood your intended point will forget your message within moments of reading it. There are just too many other sources competing for our scarce attention.

Does this mean that it is pointless to try and communicate? Not at all. My learning from the last few decades of communicating with large groups is this:

1. Keep your messages short.

2. Repeat them.

It typically takes three to five repetitions of a message before you reach a majority of the audience.

If we are honest, part of the reason no one listens to us is that we have nothing important to say.

Most of what we do as humans is fleeting and leaves no lasting impression. A conversation is one of the most fleeting of all, with even the participants in disagreement over who said what the moment the conversation is over.

One reason people get so animated in conversations is that they care what other people think. We are social animals, after all, and it bothers us when others' opinions differ from ours.

The Stoics argue that we should know our own minds and be confident in the wisdom of our decisions. Not all the advice or input we will get from our fellow persons will be accurate or appropriate.

A better way forward

I was drawn to this topic because of what I've seen in the public discourse recently. I don't know about you, but it seems to me that there are more people shouting at each other than ever before.

And ironically, the more heated the conversation, the less likely it is that anyone is being convinced, let alone influenced, by anything the other side says.

I am reminded of a saying from the Buddha, "Better than a thousand useless words is a single word that gives peace."

I can't guarantee that you will find peace by learning how to listen better. But you will find yourself having better conversations and communicating better.

Be well.

Chapter Four

Can You Freely Speak Your Mind?

Do you think you live in a country that protects freedom of speech? How about at school, at work, or on the Internet?

The questions for this chapter are, "Can you freely speak your mind?" and "Do you?" If you want to be successful in your career and life, you must be able to answer both questions with a clear "Yes."

I think many of us when asked these questions would instinctively say "Of course!" At least, I suspect you would answer this way if you live in most places in Europe or the United States. Perhaps today's article will cause you to question your conviction.

How has the Internet impacted freedom of speech?

We hear much about how we live in times of economic and technological miracles. Particularly with the rapid spread of the Internet across the globe, I assumed that freedom of speech had also been seeded far and wide.

I was wrong.

The organization Freedom House performs surveys on the level of internet freedom in 70 countries around the world. They look at things like Obstacles to Access, Limits on Content, and Violations of User Rights.

A recent report makes for depressing reading. (See Freedom on the Net 2023.) Among other findings:

- Global internet freedom declined for the 13th consecutive year, as "attacks on free expression grew more common around the world."

- Governments are using generative AI to drive disinformation campaigns: "At least 47 governments deployed commentators to manipulate online discussions in their favor."

It seems that economic and technological progress is not inevitably correlated with greater online freedom.

Looking at the ten most populous countries in the world, which together represent 59% of the global population, only the United States, is considered "Free" in terms of Internet Freedom.

- The U.S. represents just 4.2% of the global population.

- The other countries are rated either "Not Free" (China, Pakistan, and Russia), representing 23% of the global population,

- or "Partly Free," representing 32% of the population.

This paints a dark picture, so I went looking for other bastions of freedom. I found them in Europe, excluding Eastern Europe, where we find another 450 million citizens living in societies with Internet Freedom, almost 6% of the global population.

Beyond that, we can add relatively large countries like Japan, South Africa, Argentina, Canada, and Australia, together accounting for not quite 4% of the population.

What I take from these numbers is simply this: *The great majority of the world's population does not experience anything like the freedom of speech that most of us take for granted.* Our ability to access information and express our thoughts is an aberration, not the norm.

Don't rest easy if you're in a Free or Partly Free country

Even if you are lucky enough to find yourself in those havens of democratic freedom in Europe or the United States, should you rest easily? I'm not so sure.

According to Freedom House again,

> *Even in more democratic settings, including the United States and Europe, governments considered or actually imposed restrictions on access to prominent websites and social media platforms, an unproductive approach to concerns about foreign interference, disinformation, and online safety.*

Some of you will be tempted to dismiss this as fearmongering by disgruntled political minorities. I've had conversations with several people who insist that talk of censorship and self-censorship is greatly exaggerated and largely imaginary.

"I am fully free," so they tell me, "To speak my mind on any topic at any time."

I suspect these people are making the same mistake that I did before writing this article: Assuming that their personal experience is representative of the larger world.

Universities illustrate well our changed times

I'll pick one slice of society to explore the point, our universities. If there was one place where we could traditionally expect to find freedom of thought, freedom of expression, and an open environment, it would be the university.

In 2014 the University of Chicago published the "Chicago Principles," which set out the University's commitment to protect and promote free expression. In their view, "without a vibrant commitment to free and open inquiry, a university ceases to be a university."

> *In a word, the University's fundamental commitment is to the principle that debate or deliberation may not be suppressed because the ideas put forth are thought by some or even by most members of the University community to be offensive, unwise, immoral, or wrong-headed.*

This is an admirable principle that defines what freedom of expression means in practice and they seem to mean what they say.

So how do we explain the anecdotal evidence of speakers being "shouted down" or canceled for views that some students find offensive? The newspapers are peppered with such stories. Are these isolated examples or a sign of a dangerous trend?

Luckily for us, the Foundation for Individual Rights in Education has been conducting annual surveys of college students about free speech on their campuses. The 2024 survey included more than 55,000 students at 254 colleges and universities. As such, it gives us a good sense of current attitudes on free speech in the United States.

Here are some key findings from the 2024 College Free Speech Rankings:

- "More than half of students (56%) expressed worry about damaging their reputation because of someone misunderstanding what they have said or done.... Twenty percent reported that they often self-censor."

- "More than 2 in 5 students (45%) said that students blocking other students from attending a speech is acceptable to some degree, up from 37% last year."

- "[M]ore than a quarter of students (27%) said that using violence to stop a campus speech is acceptable to some degree, up from 20% last year."

I am blown away by these findings. Please read them again and consider the implications.

The University of Chicago is not the norm, but itself increasingly an outlier. The students we assume should be most open-minded are rather a self-censoring, censorious mob.

Are things any better in the workplace?

If so many students report self-censoring their views in an environment expressly committed to the freedom of expression, can we expect a different experience in the workplace?

At work, there is generally no upside to speaking your mind on non-work topics, and potentially a great downside. Namely that you may be fired or at least have a complaint filed against you by someone you've offended.

Companies are filled with what I'll call "optimists," by which I mean people who have an incentive to tell favorable stories.

- This includes people who draft budgets, submit forecasts, and fill out self-evaluations.

- It covers managers who set financial targets and employees who report on their contributions to results.

- Marketing professionals live in a world of optimistic hyperbole.

- It is a rare Board of Directors that hears an unpopular truth.

In-house lawyers are in a unique position to help

In this sea of Pollyannas the in-house lawyer faces a stark choice: Tell people what they *want* to hear or tell people what they *need* to hear.

The truth is painful. Often what the lawyer points out are harsh realities and obstacles to quick progress:

- That path is illegal, and the alternatives take more time and may cost more money.

- That behavior is inappropriate, and we must discipline the star employee.

- We are indeed subject to this new regulation, and we must spend money to ensure compliance.

You will be greatly liked if you tell people what they want to hear. You may even initially find career success by following this path because it takes time and bad luck for most legal problems and non-compliance to come to light.

I don't recommend basing your career decisions on luck.

The best lawyers are the ones who know their true value to their companies, which is to *always and only speak the truth*. When most around you say what they think will benefit them or what others want to hear, a person who only says what they believe to be true is a treasure indeed.

You must not let fear of disappointing others hold you back. Yes, you are discussing difficult situations, where something bad has happened or could happen. But it's rarely your personal fault, just the situation itself.

Speaking truth to power will bring you influence and respect

Every senior manager and CEO I know is (typically rightly) paranoid that they are getting bad information from their subordinates. One reason you see CEOs asking multiple people the same question is that they are trying to triangulate the truth through a thicket of self-interested answers.

If you tell the CEO what you think they want to hear, you will be missing a great chance to become one of their inner circle of trusted advisors.

- The CEO has plenty of potential lackeys but relatively few truth-tellers.

- If you are someone the CEO trusts will always say what you believe, they will seek out your perspective more often.

You will annoy others by being scrupulously honest. This is because, in the land of liars, the honest person is hated by those with something to hide. For example, when what you say contradicts someone who spun a different story. Or when someone gets in trouble as a result of your noting something inappropriate they did.

One important caveat: Speaking the truth does not mean you always divulge everything you know. Knowing when to speak, and to whom, i.e. exercising discretion, is also part of the successful lawyer's repertoire. The point is that *when* you speak you must be honest.

This advice holds true no matter what your job. To understand why, ask yourself this: If you live in a country where it is still possible to freely speak your mind, what do you think will happen if you do not?

Be well.

Chapter Five

Keep Your Cool

Long-term success as a senior manager requires you to keep your cool in many settings, including handling information overload and remaining calm when others have lost their cool

T here is so much to make us mad. The people who are trying to get us to spend more time online consuming their content know it.

News stories drip with disbelief and outrage. To skim through the headlines of even a non-partisan newspaper these days is to subject yourself to a heart rate workout.

The free access to information is, of course, to blame.

Why should this be so you ask? Back in the 1950s, the political scientist Herbert Simon noted that information consumes its recipients' attention:

> *a wealth of information creates a poverty of attention, and a need to allocate that attention efficiently among the overabundance of information sources that might consume it.*

In other words, because we have so much content potentially available to us at any moment, creators employ ever more fantastic methods to get us to stop on their stories.

Long-term success as a senior manager requires you to keep your cool in many settings, including the two I'll discuss here: Handling information overload and remaining calm when others have lost their cool. Let's consider both points.

Information overload

Even if you become reliably good at detecting misinformation, you still face an overwhelming amount of *legitimate* information relevant to your business.

Which regulations are the ones you need to focus on with high priority, and which can you put lower down on the list?

- There are hundreds of thousands of laws, rules, and regulations that apply to businesses in every country.

- If you are working in a multinational context, the number of applicable rules runs into the millions.

- Authorities themselves enforce these rules selectively in the sense that they give greater attention to certain topics at different times.

Authorities' priorities are driven by politics, public perception, and the gamut of emotional responses that characterize human behavior generally.

- Companies make convenient scapegoats for politicians looking to distract from their own poor performance.

- We are also seeing more countries using targeted enforcement against non-local companies for purposes of geopolitical positioning.

- The European Union's antitrust enforcement, or individual member countries' digital service taxes, are recent examples.

Amidst all this, you are bombarded with law firm and consultant advertising. Each firm tells you the issue they're hawking is the most important in the world, and that you must immediately drop everything or face humiliation and ruin.

So how to choose among many competing possible priorities? Guess correctly, and you will help your company safely navigate the complex minefield of public expectations and compliance.

Wrongly deprioritize even one significant topic, however, and you be held responsible for not "setting the right tone" and instead contributing to a culture of non-compliance.

The stakes are high, in other words, when you choose where to focus your limited attention.

Remain calm

Keep your cool. Take fear, and emotion, and excitement out of your decision-making if you can.

Hone your BS detector so that you can more easily tell when someone is selling you something that is unambiguously good for them, and only potentially good for you.

Collect reliable indicators to separate fevered headlines from real-world changes.

- Are companies in your industry taking up the topic?

- Have any peer companies found themselves in trouble?

- Do enforcement authorities have any teeth, and have they shown themselves willing to combat companies?

I read widely and considered multiple sources for every potential new issue. I wanted to see people with different perspectives and different agendas talking about it.

Over time, I learned which publications, and which authors within them, had a better track record of focusing on relevant topics. Your systems for detecting significance among much noise will vary, but you must develop and test them if you want to be more than just lucky in your career.

On to our final point, which is easy to describe: No one welcomes a panicky lawyer to their party.

In a crisis, a person who keeps their cool helps the whole team stay focused. True, you are operating under the same uncertainty, and you are feeling the same twisted gut, as the others. But you focus on what can be done, and on what the company needs to do next.

I suggest keeping calm amidst bedlam is also one of the easiest things for you to do.

- It's easy when you remember that you are simply playing a role, among the many roles you already play.

- Your role in a crisis is to be the level head, the sage counsel, the unflappable member of the team.

- Act that way, and you will not only start to feel that way, but others will believe you are that way.

And a person who keeps their cool when others are losing theirs is seriously cool. Try it and see if you don't agree with me.

Be well.

Chapter Six

Do You Want to Hear the Truth?

Although we are blind to many of our imperfections, our colleagues' vision is perfect when identifying our flaws

I an earlier chapter, I explored with you the question of Who Can Freely Speak Their Mind? Here, we tackle what may be a tougher question: Do you want to *hear* the truth?

Although this one may make you uncomfortable at times, stay with me to the end and I bet you'll feel better.

You will decide for yourself what you think. Let me lay down a few pieces of evidence that suggest to me we often just don't want to hear the truth:

- The formula for maintaining your weight is simple and widely known: Eat less and exercise. Yet diet books remain a significant chunk of total book sales, and new diets are introduced each year.

- The secret to happy relationships is no secret: Pay attention to the people closest to you, communicate well by listening more than you talk, and express your emotions in terms of how you feel and not what the other person said or did. Yet the offices of psychiatrists and marriage counselors are filled with angry couples and sad individuals.

- The path to advancing your career is open to all: Do a good job in your current job before you reach for the next, focus on continuous improvement in all areas of your life, and volunteer often while remaining open to opportunities.

- Yet of the 10 percent or so of the workforce that turns over every year, many are people frustrated that their aspirations have been thwarted. How many more remain within their companies but suffer from the same discontent?

I could go on because there are many more examples to choose from. I picked topics that we usually think of as anything but simple to demonstrate that *it is we humans that make topics complicated.*

Why? I'm not sure, but perhaps it is because we really would prefer an easier answer.

I can't lose weight because of my genes, or hormones, or because corporations make unhealthy food.

All true, but these are factors conveniently out of your control.

I am unlucky in love. Perhaps it's because my parents moved too often, and I have had to change schools once too many times. If only I had the right clothes, or haircut, or social media presence. It could be because my company expects me to work evenings and weekends — I have no life outside work!

All true, but also apparently outside your control.

I have not progressed my career, even though other, less-qualified, people are promoted ahead of me. Management is biased, and the company is not as committed to diversity as they pretend. I have to work twice as hard to get the same chances as others, and I'm tired of it!

True, true, true.

Focus on what we can control

Now, I don't want to make you feel bad by suggesting that what happens to you is your fault. Many things that happen to us are completely outside our control.

Stoic advice is for us to focus on what we *can* control. This starts with how we feel about what happens to us.

The Stoic solution is simplicity itself but because it requires self-knowledge and self-discipline, the great majority ignore it and seek salvation in external things.

Because you are here with me reading this, I am confident you are interested in expanding your self-knowledge. As such, let's explore the question of whether we want to hear the truth from another angle.

Notwithstanding how useful it can be to learn something about ourselves, how do we typically respond when someone offers us "constructive criticism" in the workplace or otherwise?

- Do we listen carefully and thank them for taking the time to give us feedback?

- Do we thoughtfully consider both the credibility of the person giving us advice and the objective validity of their advice?

Truth can be painful

If you're anything like me, that is not your instinctive response.

I have a raging monster inside me, tethered on the flimsiest of leashes. When someone offers me "feedback," I know to expect the monster to feel a flood of emotions. These range from shame, to fear, to outrage.

Through practice, I've learned to take note of these feelings (I cannot suppress them, and don't bother trying), while trying to listen carefully.

I am not yet gracious enough to thank the person at that moment for the gift of their observations, but at least I no longer try to counter their unprovoked attack by vigorously defending my virtue or letting the monster out to go on the offensive for me.

I think we don't want to hear the truth because the truth is often painful. We are none of us perfect, except perhaps in our mother's and grandmother's eyes.

Although we are blind to many of our imperfections, our colleagues' vision is perfect when identifying our flaws. Others see what we cannot.

In every other work setting, we acknowledge gaps and weaknesses and take steps to compensate. But when it comes to hearing truths about ourselves, we shy away.

Is it possible to overcome the resistance to hearing the truth about ourselves? I believe so.

I try now to ask myself two questions when confronted with feedback.

- "Does this feedback come from a person I trust?" If so, why wouldn't I listen to them now?

- And regardless of the source: "Is it possible that what this person is saying is true?" If so, should I not take it into consideration and act accordingly?

In this way, we can apply our continuous improvement principles based on what is *actually* true.

And because so few people are willing to undertake this exercise, you will find doing so is something like a superpower.

Be well.

Chapter Seven

Try Not Telling People You're an Expert

When listening to the advice of an expert, any expert, add "... but they could be wrong" to the end of their statement

H ave you ever noticed how often we answer the question "What do *you do?*" with a statement of *what we are?*

As in, "I'm a teacher," "I'm a nurse," or "I'm a lawyer." This no doubt conveys important information, which is why we do it.

But there are at least three reasons why you might not want to identify yourself by your profession:

- Unreasonable expectations,

- Clouded self-image, and

- Unwarranted assumptions.

Ironically, these are among the same reasons why people are usually proud to tout their professional credentials.

Let's explore the dichotomy, after which you can decide how you'll refer to yourself (and think of others) from now on.

Unreasonable expectations

Here's something that happens to many recent law school graduates. Upon hearing that you've passed your qualification exams, a friend or relative asks you a ridiculously specific question about a narrow area of tax or inheritance law.

When you say you don't know the answer and they are better off talking to a specialist, they say with some puzzlement and possibly suspicion, "But you're a lawyer, aren't you?"

Have you experienced something similar?

I suppose, compared to the layperson, the chances are much higher that you, the lawyer, would know the answer to a specific legal question.

But, because of the breadth of the legal field, it's unlikely the average lawyer will retain detailed knowledge about many areas beyond those they regularly use.

Or consider the poor soul who rashly identifies as a doctor in a social gathering. All too often they must field similar questions about a strange itch or recurrent dizziness because, after all, they're a doctor aren't they?

This is more than irritating to both parties in the conversation. Over time I think such exchanges can be corrosive to clear thinking.

If the people you interact with routinely come to you expecting that you know the answers to a lot of hard questions, you may be tempted not to disappoint them.

Indeed, most lawyers and doctors profess a self-confidence that is out of proportion to their actual track record. This is because compared to the layperson, the professional knows a lot. They certainly know enough to spout BS alongside good advice without anyone knowing the difference.

Others' high expectations are valuable if we force ourselves to live up to them. But beware of giving in to the temptation to believe others' expectations without doing the hard work necessary to be a real expert.

Clouded self-image

A related risk to identifying ourselves by what we say we are, rather than what we know or do, is that we get a false sense of what we are. This is because others' expectations of us shape how we see ourselves.

Take surgeons, whose self-image sometimes becomes greatly distorted over time. Not all surgeons are brain surgeons. Much of surgery is (reassuringly) repetitive and routine, making its practitioners more akin to experienced mechanics.

True, much of surgery beyond brain surgery is also difficult. But do we value the difficulty of the task itself or that human lives hang in the balance?

And does the fact that lives hang in the balance reflect solely on the difficulty of the task or also the fact that hospitals make mistakes at distressingly high rates?

I am not picking on doctors. We could talk about mistakes made by any professional group and find that they are not at all rare (even if they are less likely to be fatal).

My point with this discussion is to suggest that *professionals are people too and people are fallible*.

It is therefore risky for us to put too much stock in our own favorable press when it comes to assessing our actual performance.

Unwarranted assumptions

Professionals are presumed to be experts in their field and, as laypeople, we give them great deference. Professionals know this and come to rely upon it, even when demonstrating humility would be welcome.

The history of many professions is filled with cautionary tales of well-meaning but misguided individuals who were utterly wrong about vital topics. Medicine, psychology, economics, and even the annals of physics, are littered with the errors of our forebears.

Again, this is not to criticize any particular profession. It is to keep in mind that *professionals are just people*. Everyone is a fallible, biased, opinionated, and emotional creature.

I am reminded of the meditation practice called, "Just like me." As a way of developing compassion, the practitioner calls to mind the fact that everyone has fears, dreams, and desires and is, in many ways, "just like me."

There is another benefit to remembering that even professional experts are "just like us" in being fallible humans.

- We are less likely to be duped by credible-sounding experts trying to trick us.

- We are more likely to apply our own critical thinking to a situation and seek out additional information.

I described a while back how helpful it is to remind ourselves that *we are fallible* by adding, "But I could be wrong" to the end of our statements of belief.

My suggestion today is that when listening to the advice of an expert, any expert, add "... but *they* could be wrong" to the end of their statement.

If you want adulation, for your assumptions to go unchallenged, and to enjoy the deference reflexively awarded to experts, by all means, continue to introduce yourself as a lawyer, a doctor, or a similar expert.

But if you truly want to get better and to be recognized for your actual contributions, when asked what you do, try saying something like the following:

"Hi! My business card says I'm a — — — — — — . But I do many things in life, some better than others. And just like everyone, I'm not always an expert at everything I do."

I wonder which version of you people will come to respect and appreciate more over time.

Be well.

Chapter Eight

Can You Think Your Way to Success?

I made my aspirational list, put it aside, and didn't think of it for years. Looking back, I see that sheet of paper changed my life

I can think of many times in my own life when I firmly believed I would benefit from magical thinking or the power of thoughts alone.

The sports world is filled with elite athletes who practice visualization or mental imagery. This is the practice of imagining yourself performing the sporting activity as you would like to do it in the real world.

For example, if you have an important race coming up, you can visualize yourself performing the race in your head.

- There you are at the starting line, feeling calm, full of energy, and ready to go.

- You envision yourself clearly as you start running, with smooth and quick strides, conserving your energy.

- You imagine what you will feel and how you will respond when you notice some tiredness, or perhaps a stitch in your side.

- And look, here is how your neck, shoulders, arms, and legs will all be flowing and relaxed as you head into the final stretch.

It becomes palpable.

Using mental imagery

From Olympians on down to us average plodders, in sports as diverse as golf, weightlifting, running, or chess, studies have demonstrated the startling power of first playing out realistic scenarios in your head. *Psychology Today* writes about this mental imagery exercise.

It seems that our thoughts can produce similar mental patterns as the actions themselves. As a result, visualizing your specific performance in a specific setting can impact your later physical (and mental) performance.

Remarkable, but also easy to understand, I suppose, when we consider how important one's mental attitude is to performance.

You may have heard the phrase attributed to Henry Ford, "Whether you think you can or think you can't, you're right."

Visualization — and confidence — are key to producing the desired performance. By mentally going over your race or event, you are seeing yourself perform as you would like.

You are training yourself to "think you can" by seeing yourself do it in your head.

Mindfulness

I'll provide two more reasons why we might keep an open mind about the power of the mind to impact outcomes in the real world.

And I will wrap up by speculating on the thread tying all this together and offering my formula for how to turn thoughts and ideas into personal success.

First, some of you know I am sharing elements of Stoic philosophy in the **Pragmatic Wisdom** series. One key lesson is that one's state of mind is crucial in determining our path through life. By focusing on what we can control, and particularly on our thoughts, we can live a purposeful life.

You've probably heard the term, "mindfulness." Steering our thoughts and actions is part of what it means to be mindful. How could I embrace Stoic wisdom without at least being open to the idea that our thoughts have the power to shape our lives?

Articulate

Second, one of the spookiest things I ever did was write down on a single piece of paper a number of life goals: Personal, professional, financial, social, and fitness related.

It was Christmas break in 2006. I made the list as part of a career development exercise in which I considered my situation 10 years before, the present day, and where I wanted to be in 10 years.

I made my aspirational list, put it aside, and didn't think of it for years. Looking back, I see that sheet of paper changed my life.

Without realizing I was doing it, I started to knock off one item on the list after the other. By now I've accomplished more than 90 percent of the things on that now almost 20-year-old list.

I don't know about you, but I rarely complete task lists of any kind as well as that one. Mind you, these were not little goals. Many were so ambitious as to be almost comical to my 2006 eyes.

Some 10 years ago, I started to take out the list about once a year and update it. I'd check off goals I accomplished and add new goals. I might spend an hour on it, that's it.

I kept the original sheet of paper because it was already clear to me something magical (and kind of scary if I'm honest) was going on. I know it wasn't the piece of paper itself, but it was hard not to be superstitious.

I think writing down goals all those years ago helped me in two ways: I personally acknowledged what I wanted to achieve and I expanded the scope of what was possible for me to achieve.

Just writing down goals made them not only tangible but doable, and they became goals I thought I could achieve.

Did writing down goals cause me to pay more attention to them in the coming years and take action as a result? No doubt.

That's part of how we move beyond *knowing* an idea and *implementing* that idea. We have to take some concrete steps to move from thought to action.

The power of magical thinking

My experience suggests that even a small step may help get you started. Once you are on your way, if you just keep putting one foot in front of the other, then nothing will stop you from reaching your goals.

So go ahead and believe in your own magical thinking, so long as you take at least one step right away toward achieving your goals.

Be well.

Chapter Nine

I Miss Shaking Hands

Very belatedly, I have come to see the wisdom in my Swiss colleagues' practice of starting and ending meetings

W hen I started working in Switzerland, I was struck by what seemed like an annoying, old-fashioned custom.

In most business settings, a person joining a meeting is expected to individually greet each person in the room. You would say hello, shake each person's hand, and perhaps give the three cheek kisses to women, left, right, left.

And you were not done with the ceremony. Upon departure, the proper procedure is to once again shake the hand of each person in the meeting. You can understand why I soon learned to come to meetings early and leave late.

Does this seem anachronistic to you? I resisted. I never got comfortable with cheek kisses, which requires a European flair and elegance I do not possess.

Although the custom waned, with the advent of the #MeToo movement, I advised management that cheek kisses were not OK anymore. (Did I have my own ulterior motive in relegating check kisses to the compliance bad list? Maybe.)

As to the procession of handshakes, for some time I tried an airy wave at larger groups of people instead of individual greetings. This was probably an unwelcome move by a relative newcomer to a country.

Then again, as a stranger in a strange land, my colleagues probably had but minimal expectations for me.

Why the handshake is so important

The Swiss themselves are resoundingly successful in doing business in foreign countries.

I sense they hold themselves to a high standard, from learning the local language to spending time understanding and following local customs and practices.

Plunk a good Swiss manager down almost anywhere in the world, and he or she will thrive. I saw this over and over again, and I am deeply impressed.

The common thread between the handshake ceremony and success in foreign settings may be a simple acknowledgment of, and respect for, others as individuals.

- You hear Americans described as individualistic, and I agree.

- But the difference is that Americans prioritize themselves as *individuals*, while Swiss customs indicate they value *others*.

It is certainly both acknowledgment and respect to take a moment to shake each person's hand. Maybe this helps set the tone for productive meetings because each person feels individually welcomed. You are there for your personal attributes and so you feel more comfortable contributing.

The contracting process helped me evaluate the importance of handshakes.

I'm not ashamed to admit I love contracting and I hope I've gotten good at it. I've certainly had a lot of practice, overseeing more than 10 million commercial agreements. Of course, only a tiny fraction of those had in-depth review and negotiation, but it's still a big number.

I started teaching contracting principles to Master of Law students several years ago. When I was creating materials, I thought about how businesspeople make deals and have done so for centuries.

- You signal agreement by shaking hands. The handshake represents so much more, though.

- On an individual level, it signals trust, personal commitment, and a certain responsibility for the relationship going forward.

Honor the spirit of an agreement even if legally you could challenge it

In observing my business colleagues in practice, I realized that handshakes are powerful.

If a person agrees to something and shakes hands on it, the agreement becomes more meaningful than the strict enforceability of the words from a legal perspective.

This translates into better contract drafting by following a simple principle: Always ask for what you want, and make sure the business parties acknowledge what's been agreed upon, with a signature or a handshake, or both.

An example: It was important to me that we limited our liability when selling our products. I wanted to use the same simple and clearly written contract clause in all jurisdictions, even though in some countries this was not always enforceable as written.

However, we found that our business partners almost always honored the spirit of the agreement even though they could have made a legal argument challenging its enforceability.

Why? Because we could say to them, we had a deal. You signed the agreement (handshake or not), and the deal is clear. The lawyers in the background would make their arguments, but the business sense, the unwritten honor code, usually prevailed.

Connect with others

I hope you agree there are many solid business reasons to respect the handshake. It took the pandemic to drive home how important the handshake is on a personal level as well.

How many times did you catch yourself holding out your hand in greeting or farewell, only to realize that social distancing forbids it? I did this over and over, and it made me realize that the handshake is key to forming emotional bonds.

You like people more, and they like you more, when you make a connection. Yes, we can still do this with words remotely, but a handshake is simple, quick, and effective.

I miss handshakes, and I look forward to their return.

Very belatedly, I have come to see the wisdom in my Swiss colleagues' practice of starting and ending meetings. The next time I go to a meeting, I will gladly shake everyone's hand.

Just don't expect me to kiss anyone.

Be well.

Chapter Ten

Observations From a Social Media Noob

If you find yourself connecting with the majority of your audience, feel free to ignore the small and grouchy minority

H ave you ever noticed that the professionals most likely to attract interest on social media are often the least inclined to use it?

I am thinking of business owners and senior executives who have fantastic experience and know-how that others would love to hear about. The problem? They're usually so focused on their priorities, and so busy in general, that they spend little or no time on social media.

That was me not long ago. I spent the first 25 years of my career almost entirely focused on the job in front of me. When I went in-house, I saw the value in interacting with other in-house lawyers, so became active in ACC. Good call. As much enjoyment as I got out of the interactions, I could justify them by the business benefit I got from meeting with peers.

As for social media, I barely gave it a moment's thought. I created a Facebook profile and then largely deleted it because of privacy concerns. I think I went more than a decade without once logging in. Later I set up a LinkedIn profile — isn't that what professionals do? —and then let it languish.

At least I would check in on LinkedIn every couple of months and, if someone I knew sent me an invitation to connect, I would accept. I think I created my first post in 2021, although I've since gotten quite a bit more active. Still, when I tell you I doubled my connections in the last year you should not be impressed.

Being relatively new to the game, I have been carefully observing how others behave, what seems to work well, and what gets people in trouble. I think I've identified some parallels to other professional pursuits that may shed some light on basic human nature. Understanding this, perhaps we can improve our performance not just on social media but in other areas of our jobs and our lives.

I've still got questions, though. Maybe you can help me understand.

Is it possible to post anything of substance without attracting detractors?

In my experience, a certain percentage of people simply disagree with you, no matter what point you're making. (I'm not talking about cat videos or people-are-amazing clips. Everyone loves those.) Looking at polls from Rasmussen Reports over the last few years, it seems around 25 percent of those polled reliably express downright bizarre opinions.

This is consistent with something I noticed when I started teaching about 10 years ago. I would prepare diligently for my classes and tried hard to be informative and entertaining. I watched other great lecturers and applied continuous improvement principles. And yet, no matter the topic or the class, I would simply not click with maybe 10 percent of the group, sometimes more.

Could it be me?

Yes, of course, there could be style I could adopt that would click with the other 10 percent or so of the class. But seeing the phenomenon now repeated in other domains, whether I'm trying to be serious or funny, supportive or critical, I've come to believe that perfect communication with 100 percent of your audience is simply impossible.

Repeating my classes over multiple years helped me realize it might not entirely be my fault. That's because the critical feedback from year to year differs significantly, even though I deliver the same (or hopefully continuously better) lectures. This is not surprising when you think about it. From psychology we know that people are emotional, irrational, biased, and suffer routinely from cognitive dissonance.

At any moment, a certain percentage of any large group is going to see the same story unfold but take away a very different meaning.

As a result, I've learned to expect dissonant responses on social media, and I don't let it bother me. Well, at least I try. It helps me when I remember that many more readers are either neutral or positive than will ever let you know. In other words, there are many viewers who silently appreciate your point. I've had many conversations with colleagues and been happily surprised when they refer to a post or an article they saw. I didn't know they were there.

What is the ratio of lurkers to posters?

I think lurkers, or passive viewers to make it seem less creepy, outnumber posters by at least 10 to one. And of the posters, a small but vocal minority who feel passionate about certain topics often dominate the public space. Let's posit that one percent is grouchy, nine percent positive, and 90 percent silent.

You will measure your communication effectiveness your own way. But don't be too hard on yourself. If you find yourself connecting with the majority of your audience, feel free to ignore the small and grouchy minority. One of the very best things I learned on Facebook was the power of blocking people determined to be jerks. I've only had to use it once, but the benefit to my wellbeing was immediate.

If only I could find a way to do the same in real life.

Be well.

Chapter Eleven

Swiss Cheese Your Way to Safety

Any in-house counsel worth their salary knows that learning from the mistakes of others is free tuition in the school of life

H as your company ever gone through a serious problem or crisis? If you have *not yet* dealt with such wrenching times, you should prepare now.

If you have experienced the pain of a compliance failure, you likely want to learn more about the best way to handle it. And you are surely motivated to ensure similar mishaps don't happen again.

Any in-house counsel worth their salary knows that learning from the mistakes of others is free tuition in the school of life. Knowing the pitfalls, however, is the easy part.

Getting people to pay sufficient attention to potential problems before they arise is much harder. Or, as I've said elsewhere, "We do not lack for knowledge of what to do, we lack the will to do it."

I'll help you find the will to act by making your task easier.

While serious problems in companies can arise without warning as a result of single acts, such instances are thankfully rare. We don't need to spend much time on them because, for truly one-off failures, it's difficult to anticipate them so challenging to maneuver in advance.

Most significant problems are the result of multiple issues

In my experience, most significant problems are born of multiple causes in the sense that they result from several, cascading failures.

Often one or more of these failures sets off warning signals to vigilant watchers. The first lesson: Be aware of any signs of crisis considered averted.

When one of your monitoring systems nips an issue in the bud, be thankful. But look carefully at what allowed the risk to arise at all. Something is not right.

Small problems by definition don't cause significant harm. It's tempting therefore to ignore them to focus on bigger issues. But small problems have a way of growing when you're not looking.

A mantra I repeated often with my team was: "Don't let small problems become big problems." So study your small problems and understand root causes wherever possible.

In diagnosing your non-catastrophic failures, consider what standards of behavior you expect of your colleagues.

Do you expect employees to first remember all relevant rules and then to understand and follow them correctly at all times? If so, you may be new to the job. (Or you may have better colleagues than I did; I liked mine a lot despite their failings.)

So, we need to assume that people are imperfect. They will be distracted, make mistakes, and sometimes try to subvert our systems. Although people are wonderful as individuals, in groups they are predictably and depressingly unreliable.

Some people, perhaps most people, will not follow all the rules all of the time. People make exceptions for themselves and happily refuse to follow rules they don't agree with.

The Swiss cheese strategy

If we expect mistakes and noncompliance from the start, we can design our systems to anticipate them.

For one, we pay more attention to incentives. Can we design incentives to directly encourage the behavior we want and discourage otherwise expected but unwanted behavior?

Further, we usually seek to build in redundant protections, assuming that one or even several layers of defense may be insufficient. And in redundancy lies the Swiss cheese strategy.

Simply put, consider each of your defenses as a slice of Swiss cheese* in the sense that it has holes in it. Each slice of your compliance system will stop some problems, but not all.

So you layer on another slice of cheese, aligned slightly differently, which stops many of the issues that made it through the first line of defense.

But again, perhaps not all. So you add a third slice of cheese.

Take your contracting process as an example of the strategy in operation:

- You will have carefully prepared standard terms and conditions, and maybe some standard agreements, the first line of defense. But you won't be able to use your agreement in every transaction.

- So then you prepare a contracting guideline as a second layer. Your guideline sets out in simple and clear terms the must-haves and nice-to-haves in every deal. But your team won't negotiate every point successfully and will make exceptions.

- As a third line of defense, you may require nonstandard terms to be approved by successive layers of management. The approval requirement serves two purposes: It means teams try harder to get compliant terms to avoid having to ask for approval and it gives management a chance to influence the deal.

The beauty of this system is that each of the individual defenses may be simple and inexpensive. After all, they don't need to be perfect. Just add another simple and inexpensive layer. Simple systems are easier to explain and implement, meaning you get less resistance.

The Swiss cheese approach of layering redundant and backup systems greatly reduces the chances that one or a series of small problems will grow into something catastrophic.

And here you thought the Swiss just melted their cheese.

Be well.

* My Swiss friends are yelling at the screen now saying, "There are literally hundreds of types of Swiss cheese! What do you mean 'Swiss cheese'?" To an American's eyes, not to mention taste, Swiss cheese usually means something resembling Emmental, with large yellow slices containing eyes or holes.

Chapter Twelve

Dealing with One-Issue Stakeholders

For your stakeholders to stop shouting and listen to you, they must feel that you have listened to and understood them

I n the corporate world, we often encounter stakeholders who care deeply about a particular issue.

These stakeholders use their focus and passion to drive attention to their topic. They write letters to regulators and the board, file shareholder proposals, and generate publicity, all of which create pressure on companies to act.

In-house counsel and their companies are at a disadvantage when dealing with such vocal advocates. The advocates have just one issue, and they are willing to do almost anything to promote their cause.

We, in contrast, have hundreds of issues to deal with, and many pressing priorities. We simply do not have as much time to devote to the topic as they do.

When confronted with one-issue stakeholders, no one cares as much as *they* do about *their* issue.

I don't want to digress today into the debate about whether companies should be primarily shareholder-focused or stakeholder-focused. It's sufficient to observe that the stakeholder model suffers from a serious defect.

Namely, there is no consistent and accepted mechanism for deciding priorities among competing stakeholder interests. Hence, the shouting we see among stakeholders to make the most noise, so companies pay heed to their squeaky wheel.

How should a company react?

When all the wheels are squeaking all the time, what is a responsible company to do?

One answer is to simply ignore the noise and develop your strategy top-down, quietly, without being influenced by externalities. After all, management and the board surely know best what the company's strengths and weaknesses are, and where the most promising opportunities lie.

The risk here is that by ignoring stakeholders you only arouse them to greater heights of frenzy. What do people do when they think someone has not heard their message? They repeat it, and more stridently each time.

True, sometimes they get tired or veer off to pursue a more receptive target. But particularly with passionate stakeholders, and that's most of them, ignoring a stakeholder request in favor of your own priorities is a risky path.

So, what to do?

Listen

Listening to stakeholders is a good idea, even though it can seem like a waste of time.

True, we already understand the issue well because we've heard it many times before. Listen, nonetheless. You might still learn something new.

More importantly, by listening you take away the stakeholder's immediate need to escalate.

You can make even more progress if you then acknowledge the importance of the topic. Perhaps you will express your desire to see positive change.

For your stakeholder to stop shouting and listen to you, they must feel that you have listened to and understood them. A stakeholder is someone who has an interest in, and is affected by, the company's decisions. So, it is right to listen to and genuinely seek to understand their concerns.

Only now are you in a position to safely raise the issue of competing priorities. But be careful.

In my experience, it never goes over well when you say some issues are more important than others. Even though this is demonstrably true, no one wants to hear that their issue is not the most important one. A disappointed stakeholder is likely to take out their frustration on you, the messenger.

Focus on the impact your company can have

What I've found works better is to focus on the *impact* your company can have. That is, where can you make a substantive difference?

Preserving access to clean water is no doubt important, but if you are a software development company you may have less of an impact here than, say, a mining company. Explain what areas you are focused on, and why.

The conversation goes something like this:

Stakeholder: *Passionate advocacy, i.e., request for your company to immediately and completely change its business model and upend everything that made it successful.*

Company (calmly): *Thank you for raising your concern. We hear you and understand your issue. We agree that [topic] is an important and relevant issue that the world needs to tackle.*

Our company is focused on X, Y, and Z of the UN Sustainable Development Goals [or similar]. We focus on these particular areas because, given the nature of our business, the location of our operations, and the partners we work with, we feel these are the areas where can have the greatest impact.

Environmental, social, and governance (ESG) strategy

It helps if you have already publicly described your environmental, social, and governance (ESG) strategy and can refer back to it in the conversation. Your strategy will outline where you can have the greatest impact and, thus, where your focus areas are.

If you have not developed and published an ESG strategy, I can only recommend you do so. Otherwise, you are at great risk of a one-issue stakeholder dragging you to their level and defeating you with their persistence.

Be well.

Chapter Thirteen

No One Cares as Much as You Do

Your ambitions exceed your abilities not because of any failing on your part, but because everyone is focused on their own priorities

I will tell you why you need to be a one-issue stakeholder if you want to be successful. The reason is that no one cares as much as *you* do about *your* issues.

This rule applies universally across your entire life. It operates at work and in your personal life. On every topic you can think of, you care the most about the things that affect you.

Everyone else is a one-issue stakeholder

Your doctor may be wonderful, talented, and caring. You are still one of hundreds of patients, and for the doctor, there is a commercial aspect to your visit that colors the encounter. Thus, you must be your own zealous advocate in managing your health.

Your contractor is a whiz with every kind of power tool, sticks to their quotes, and answers the phone. You are still one of many clients, and for the contractor, your project is a job to be completed and an invoice to be paid. They do not have to live in the house after the renovation and will not notice every fleck and imperfection the way you will.

Your kid's teacher is patient, experienced, and magic with the class. Your child is one of a room full of students, and for the teacher represents a source of work and aggravation. There is homework to review and tests to correct, but the end of term looms with graduation all but certain. Whether your child performs to her maximum potential is no doubt a matter of some interest, but no teacher's concern will match your own when it comes to your child.

What does it mean, practically?

I don't mean to depress you by hammering home the point. Understanding that no one cares as much as you do about your issue gives rise to two important implications:

1. Implementing your initiative (say writing consistently and growing your followers organically) requires *much* more effort than you think it should.

2. You can successfully pursue fewer initiatives than you would like at any given time, also due to the first point. This is because you'll be spending more time and effort driving progress on each initiative.

Why success is elusive ... but approachable

Your ambitions exceed your abilities not because of any failing on your part, but because everyone is focused on their own priorities. Be realistic, therefore, in your expectations of how quickly you will advance in pushing your priorities. There is no shortcut. There are no exceptions.

Take your talent and your energy and devote them to being a tireless advocate for one (or a few) initiatives at a time. And then plan on doing it over and over again for everything in your life that you consider important.

If you find this image disheartening, let me leave you with this thought to cheer you up again.

- Each time you persist and persevere, you will become more effective.

- You'll learn which of your strengths to leverage in what settings, and which of your counterparts respond best to what pressure.

- Your tasks become easier, therefore, whenever you succeed.

Your colleagues will not be as patient as you. They will mistake busyness and effort for progress, although these are not the same. You will recognize that only progress is progress, no matter the desire and effort. Because of this, you will succeed more often.

Over time, the combination of your focus, persistence, and successful implementation makes you unstoppable. That is worth fighting for.

So go ahead and care about your issues, the more the better.

Be well.

Chapter Fourteen

Identifying Problems Worth Working On

What can you do that no one else will do, or do as well?

L et me start with a fundamental truth that experienced employees know all too well: Identifying problems is easy.

New employees are typically astounded at how many problems they quickly identify when starting a new job.

Guess what? You are not the first person or the only person to detect things that aren't working perfectly. I tell new hires that identifying problems is the easiest thing for an employee to do.

If you stop at merely identifying problems, you won't be much use to your colleagues or your company.

Employees who go on to add real value become just as adept at proposing solutions to the problems they identify. But, as we'll discuss in Identifying Solutions That Will Work (the following chapter), it turns out that *proposing solutions* is also not the hard part.

Driving change is the hard part

The hard part in driving change is as follows: Identifying which problems are worth focusing on, and which solutions are worth pursuing among many possible approaches.

Doing so requires a blend of strategic thinking and real-world pragmatism that most people only gain through experience. Let me explain why this is so.

We typically have a rich buffet of problems always laid out before us. Faced with this abundance, many people choose to address problems they feel are manageable. That is, smaller problems with relatively quick solutions.

Is someone requesting your input via email? That's easy. Take a few minutes and respond to them. This type of problem-solving can be quite satisfying. You are checking items off your list and making visible progress.

The typical workday also requires us to deal with mundane topics. Few people can avoid the many minor interactions that make up modern work.

Hence, the abundance of advice we see on how to work more efficiently. If we are going to spend a fair amount of time dealing with little problems, it is useful for us to learn how to solve them quickly and well.

The expedient path to problem-solving is nonetheless a risky path.

Notice first how the number of small problems never diminishes. Each task we accomplish provides a fleeting burst of pleasure but is rewarded by two more tasks.

Next notice how often we spend our entire day in a succession of what we thought would be brief moments of quick answers. The many little things we chase after mindlessly eat up the day.

Focus on what can make the greatest difference

If you are purposeful, you may have carefully thought about your important priorities. These are the strategic things that you believe will have the greatest influence.

Ask yourself how much overlap there is between the small daily problems you usually spend time on and your strategic priorities. If you are like most people I know, the answer is not much.

Another risk is that the further you advance in your career, the more you will find people looking for you to help solve *their* urgent problems.

This is only natural, but you must be aware of this key fact: Other people's problems are not necessarily your problems. And helping solve other people's problems is often not the best use of your time.

If solving other people's problems is not the best use of your time, do you have a clear sense of what is? Take a moment and write down what you think are among your greatest potential contributions to your company. How do you (or can you) add value?

Your greatest value may be that you helped avoid problems

Especially for lawyers, keep in mind that your greatest contribution may be avoiding negative outcomes.

People overweight additive initiatives, like acquisitions, introducing new products, or entering new territories. But, often, tremendous value hides in helping ensure your company and colleagues do not, pardon the phrase, f — things up.

We know there is great value in strong governance and effective compliance. But our business colleagues do not default to preventive measures unless prompted.

Summary and method

In sum, problems large and small always clamor for our attention. The things we spend time on by default may be a necessary part of our day, but they are unlikely to be the most important problems.

It is helpful for us to carefully consider the ways in which we add value because this helps us identify potential problems worth focusing on.

I recommend taking the process in separate stages.

First, devote quality time to identifying a long list of problems that your team or your company is facing.

- At this stage, just identify problems.

- Try hard not to consider how easy each problem would be to solve, but rather rank them according to how valuable it would be if they were solved.

Then put your list of problems aside and consider the ways in which you add value.

- What can you do that no one else will do, or do as well?

- Your contribution may be in the form of focusing on things others do not, being willing to devote more time to a project, or in the special skills and abilities you possess or can nurture.

Now you are ready to take your short list of potentially strategic problems and match it up against your list of your unique value propositions.

If you're lucky, this will reveal a few overlaps where you would be well-positioned to focus your efforts.

Be well.

Chapter Fifteen

Identifying Solutions That Will Work

I've seen talented managers devise solutions that would unquestionably address a strategic problem but still fail to make progress

B efore we consider solutions to problems, we need to evaluate which problems are worth our attention. I discussed this in the prior chapter.

Although we are tempted to pursue problems with quick solutions, we create enduring value by focusing instead on strategic problems. This essay addresses how to devise effective solutions to our strategic problems.

Just as with identifying problems, proposing solutions is easy. You are not the first person or the only person to come up with any number of solutions to the problems you've identified.

Here's the thing: Strategic problems typically have no easy solutions. They wouldn't be strategic problems otherwise.

I've seen talented, successful managers devise solutions that would unquestionably address a strategic problem but still fail to make progress. Why is this?

Otherwise promising solutions fail for many reasons, most prominently:

1. Underestimating historical and cultural factors supporting the status quo, and

2. Focusing too much on the benefits without considering the costs.

Let's explore both points.

Figure out what caused the problem

Before we can safely dive into problem-solving mode, it is critical to ask how the situation developed and why.

Although some problems develop spontaneously, there are very often explanations behind the things that appear screwed up to us today. It helps to understand how we got here before trying to set a path to a new destination.

Change requires effort, and significant change requires extraordinary effort.

Because people are creatures of habit, we tend to keep doing what we have been doing, even if we know it's expensive, inefficient, or downright harmful. Ask anyone who has tried to change their eating, exercise, or spending habits.

The burden of change today is magnified when the reward is distant in time. The more we must change for a speculative future reward, the harder the challenge.

Thus, the first reason potential solutions fail is that we don't account sufficiently for human stubbornness, which tends to preserve the status quo. The obvious correctness of a solution doesn't help overcome this.

In a work setting, successful implementation means you must be willing to either (1) invest extraordinary effort in pushing your solution, or (2) identify and piggyback on existing initiatives and cultural currents underlying the behavior you want to change.

Determine who can help you implement the needed change

Even if you can invest extraordinary effort, you are well-served to spend time understanding your company's culture.

- Who among your colleagues has a respected voice and will support you?

- Are there other successful initiatives already underway to which you can add your own initiative?

Think of your company as a slow-moving river of molasses. Don't try to push your boat against the flow, or uphill. You may be able to gradually shift the course, but remember you are dealing with incredible momentum.

Now to the second reason solutions fail, which is not sufficiently considering the costs. These costs include the active resistance from those who are disadvantaged by upsetting the status quo and the unintended consequences our solution gives rise to.

It is because of these factors that even successful projects regularly take twice as long and cost twice as much as planned.

Plan ahead for obstacles and how to circumvent what you can

You can forecast likely costs more accurately by conducting pre-mortems. That is, assume your project has failed (or stalled, or taken longer, or cost more, etc.). Now describe all the reasons why.

This will help you plan for those obstacles, and perhaps avoid some of them. But mostly it will help you come up with a more realistic assessment of what substantive change behind your initiative will require.

You should be sobered, if not depressed, upon concluding your pre-mortem exercise.

Significant change requires extraordinary effort, which comes at the cost of all the other things you cannot pursue. If you are grand in your expectations, be humble at least in your estimate of how quickly you will proceed.

Know the costs of the solution

Recognize that when we push solutions without a clear understanding of costs, we do worse than impede progress. We lose time and waste resources pursuing solutions that are bound to fail, making an eventual effective solution that much harder to implement.

I'll end with an example to illustrate the dynamic. Most people agree that human-caused climate change is a serious, global concern. The solutions seem obvious to policymakers: Immediately and drastically cut carbon emissions, while shifting to renewable energy.

A short reflection using our new model reveals, however, why the obvious solutions are destined for failure.

- We have not given enough weight to the historical context: particularly that today's first-world economies developed on the back of low-cost energy delivered by fossil fuels. Today's developing economies are naturally interested in their own advancement, which cannot be accomplished cost-effectively with renewables.

- Consumers in many countries have grown accustomed to their current quality of life, which has been fueled by decades of steady or declining energy prices. Achieving net-zero carbon emissions requires immediate cost and real sacrifice for the foreseeable future in return for a very long-term, speculative payoff.

- Should we assume that most people will suddenly decide to put future generations' interests above their own? I suppose coordinated altruistic behavior by large groups of people is possible, but it goes against all historical precedents.

Climate change may well be the most important project for the world to work on. I predict we won't make great progress until we are considerably more transparent about the costs.

Only then will individuals and societies be willing to consider whether the costs are worth the benefits. Importantly, seeing the true extent of the costs will trigger a search for alternative solutions that may be equally effective but easier to implement.

Being transparent about costs is one of the best ways you can improve the quality of your problem-solving. Showing true costs seems risky, but the payoff may be a solution that works. That's worth taking a risk for.

Be well.

Chapter Sixteen

Why It's So Hard Being a Good Corporate Lawyer

Even if you're not a lawyer, pity for a moment the career path they are facing

I f you want to become a good in-house lawyer (that is, a lawyer who works for a corporation) you face a number of problems. Let me depress you for a few minutes by describing what some of those problems are:

Law school didn't teach you practical skills

To start with, your law school did not teach you many practical skills and tools necessary to be effective. Here's a quote from the New York State Bar Association Task Force on the Future of the Legal Profession:

We used to think that being a good lawyer simply meant knowing the law. Today, we are more likely to think that good lawyers know how to do useful things with the law to help solve client problems. — New York State Bar Association Task Force on the Future of the Legal Profession

So it's not enough to know the law; you have to know how to *do* useful things with it to solve your organization's problems.

Now, the law school method of how to teach someone to become a lawyer is largely unchanged for the last 150 years. I hope we'd all agree that the practice of at least in-house counsel has moved on since then.

Law firms and bar associations believe law schools should pick up the slack, not them.

But for the sake of argument, let's say law schools are doing what they should because someone has to teach you about the substantive law, and how to think analytically.

Law firms can't prepare you for in-house life

Your next problem is what happens after you graduate from law school. Let's assume you start working at a law firm. Law firms are good at many things but law firms simply don't know everything that an in-house counsel needs to know.

There are entire areas of skills that are relevant in-house that are not relevant in a law firm. And as we've seen, they don't think it's their job to train lawyers for in-house practice.

So you won't get your in-house training in a law firm either.

You can't count on high-quality company training

Now let's assume you've made the switch to a company, government agency, or another organization, and you're actually practicing in-house. All clear, right?

Unfortunately, your search is not over because it is a rare organization that trains its in-house counsel in a systematic way across all disciplines that might be relevant. What training exists is either ad hoc or narrowly focused.

- Ad hoc training often takes place in smaller teams that don't have the resources to do systematic training.

- And in the bigger organizations that do have training resources, lawyers often become specialized, so your exposure to broad issues is limited.

You'll learn most by doing

What this means is that most of your learning is on-the-job training, or learning by doing. This can be very good indeed but, under the *best of circumstances*, it can take years and years of experience to become truly effective as in-house counsel

— at least from the perspective of having broad awareness and skills across many topics, i.e., being a corporate generalist.

Ultimately, whether you become a well-rounded generalist who is capable of not just handling the daily work but anticipating challenges and strategically planning ahead is largely a matter of luck. The right organization, the right team, the right time, etc.

With this depressing background out of the way, how do you improve your odds of getting ahead? Here's my personal view: The best thing you can do is to become highly valuable to your organization starting with what you're doing right now.

In other words, do such a good job where you are with what's in front of you that your legal team, your business colleagues, and everyone you interact with, all think "Now there's a person I'd want to work with again if I ever got a chance."

In the next few chapters, I am going to lay bare my best secrets on how to outperform at work as part of a series on **Master Skills for Communicating at Work**.

You can cut to the front of the line

Although it took me years of experiment and practice to develop this guidance, I want you to cut right to the front of the line. Why am I sharing these secrets with you? It's because I saw the wonderful impact they can have on a company and its culture.

- Initially, I saw the benefit among my team members, who became some of our most appreciated employees.

- The interesting thing was when people saw how effective our communication practices were, they clamored to have them spread across the company.

It's because I know how hard your job is and appreciate how much you do that I want to help you be more effective.

Stay tuned.

Be well.

Chapter Seventeen

The Day You Became Smarter

Part of the Master Skills series on how to crush your job with better communication — five tips to write clearly

I wasted a decade or more sharpening my legal skills until I realized the secrets to great performance lay elsewhere.

And they weren't even hard to learn.

I'd like to spare you that lost time and share the secrets. This and the next several chapters comprise the Master Skills on how to communicate better.

- Write plainly and clearly (this chapter)

- Taming the email monster (Write Better Emails Today)

- Avoiding time-wasting meetings (Maybe Don't Go to that Meeting)

- Influencing others (Persuade Like Aristotle)

- Engaging with others (Listen Up Already)

If you want your work colleagues to be amazed at how much smarter you've become overnight, **write everything in plain language** that everyone can understand.

Lawyers are notoriously bad communicators

Although this advice applies to any manager, it is particularly helpful for lawyers.

Why is that? Because our non-lawyer colleagues expect us to be confusing, poor communicators. We're famous for our impenetrable legalese.

When you show up with your simple and clear messages, you will stun people. They will understand what you're saying. Because of this, they will think you're brilliant, far out of proportion to your actual legal chops.

Do you know how a layperson determines which of two people is the better lawyer? One or more of these factors typically comes into play:

- A better-looking suit;

- Billing at a higher hourly rate than competitors;

- The lawyer lets slip that they graduated from Harvard or Yale;

- They return calls; and

- They can string together a comprehensible sentence.

For years, I thought the secret was returning calls. Colleagues so appreciate responsiveness that it really seemed like a genius way to generate goodwill. And it is.

But it's not enough if you also want people to think you're smart.

You probably know this, but in-house lawyers must never rely on the first three factors because they all serve as barriers to our business colleagues liking us.

Although Machiavelli assured us in The Prince it is better to be feared than loved, being liked is a good middle ground. This means your path to legal stardom lies in being a great communicator.

For our purposes, let me modify Machiavelli with the following five rules for clear writing:

1. It is better to be understood than complete

You spent a long time becoming a legal expert. Don't show off all that you know. Don't go down every hypothetical pathway for the sake of completeness. Start with the most likely scenario and describe it simply.

Being understood also means you use simple words and omit extra words. I love words and I know lots of fancy ones. But simple words get your point across better.

Short sentences work better than longer ones. Same for short paragraphs.

2. It is better to be kind than precise

This means knowing your audience and giving them just what they need.

How much detail must you give for a reader to understand the point? Sure, you had to look up all sorts of laws and regulations to answer the question, but does it help your reader when you list them chapter and verse? Normally not.

If you think some readers may want more detail, offer it in later sections or even an appendix. The reader who is interested in the detail can continue, while the ones who trust your answer can stop.

3. It is better to be first than last

What I mean is this: Make your last sentence into your first sentence. Nothing demonstrates a stellar communicator so much as starting with the answer or conclusion.

I know that's not how lawyers' minds work. We start with the facts, determine the relevant law, perform an analysis, and only then come to our conclusion.

Keep right on doing that. But once you've reached the end of your analysis, simply move your concluding sentence up to the top, and you'll go from average lawyer to superstar in one easy stroke.

4. It is better to be active than passive

You should give every sentence a subject. Don't hide behind ambiguity.

I know sometimes we don't know who the actor is. But we lawyers have let the passive voice take over all our writings. And the passive voice does more than make our sentences dull. People don't understand passive sentences as well.

Our bad habit is deeply ingrained. I encourage you to root it out, sentence by sentence.

Good news for everyone who can't stop from writing in the passive voice right away: You can more easily spot passive sentences upon a second reading. That leads us to our final point.

5. It is better to edit than write perfectly

I told you upfront the secret to good communication wasn't hard to learn. Knowing the secret doesn't mean you will write perfectly all the time.

Despite years of practice, I catch myself reverting to old habits often. The solution is to read and edit what you write, which thankfully is much easier than writing perfectly.

Simply check your next document against these five rules and you'll be a better writer than almost all your colleagues.

And you can bask in their amazement at how much smarter you've suddenly become.

Be well.

PS — I was inspired to write this by two brilliant sources on clear writing; I hope you go on to inspire your colleagues by your example: The US Security and Exchange Commission's Plain English Handbook (including the preface by Warren Buffet), which contains numerous tips that are useful no matter what language you use, and Scott Adam's blog, The Day You Became A Better Writer.

Chapter Eighteen

Write Better Emails Today

Part of the Master Skills series on how to crush your job with better communication — ten tips for better emails

J ust to mention it, maybe you shouldn't write so many emails.

I share below how to make your emails awesome but that assumes you need to write one at all. Sometimes you don't.

You know emails are terrible for emotionally charged situations. Did you also know that the best predictor of how many emails a person receives is how many they send?

If you find yourself plagued with emails, consider the anti-Nike approach: Just don't do it.

But I get it. Emails are unavoidable, often necessary, and sometimes useful.

When I managed a global legal team, I loved being able to pass on assignments at the end of my day knowing that colleagues half a day behind me (or ahead) would still have time to handle them. I imagined that the sun never set on our hard-working team.

Allowing for asynchronous communication, as in I write when I have time and you respond when you have time, permits us both to maximize our productivity.

Thus, I start with the premise that you must write at least some emails. So, let's write the best possible emails, shall we?

10 Secrets to Better Emails

1. Use clear subject lines

Your subject line should describe the topic and whether the message is for information only or whether action is required. Edit outdated or unclear subject lines when you respond to emails you receive.

2. State your purpose early

The very first sentence of your message should tell readers what you want from them.

If you are requesting specific action or follow-up, make sure the deliverable is clear.

3. Set deadlines

Always set a deadline and highlight it in bold or another color. Be realistic in setting deadlines, recognizing that your colleagues have other priorities.

4. Only include necessary information

Give only the background information or context necessary for your reader to understand your message, no more.

Delete unnecessary text, including prior messages, as appropriate.

5. Avoid jargon

Do not use legalese, terms of art, acronyms, or other abbreviations that your reader may not know.

6. Have a good review process

Review the content of your message to ensure it is short, simple, and focused.

Consider asking a colleague to review important messages to check they are clear.

7. Keep your distribution narrow

Have a specific reason for each person you send your message to. Only send emails to persons who must act on the message.

The broader your distribution, the less likely an individual reader feels it was intended for them.

8. Separate emails to smaller groups

If you have to send emails to a lot of recipients, consider sending multiple individual emails to smaller, relevant groups of people.

9. Keep emails to five sentences or fewer

Challenge yourself to write concisely. See five.sentenc.es/ for inspiration. It's not always possible, but the challenge of reducing a long reply to five sentences helps clarify your key points. You can usually eliminate a lot.

These tips are powerful because people can implement them easily. You just have to want to do it and then be mindful of what you are doing.

Thus, I will end with my final tip for writing better emails:

10. Don't hit send before reviewing your emails against this checklist

It is hard to write emails perfectly the first time. But editing them is easy.

I wish you happy editing.

Be well.

Chapter Nineteen

Maybe Don't Go to that Meeting

Part of the Master Skills series on how to crush your job with better communication — ten tips for awesome meetings

N othing sends a signal that you carefully manage your time like declining a meeting invitation. Short of just saying no, which I understand will be a shock in many organizations, how about asking what you would be there for:

I see you invited me to meeting X. Based on the agenda, I am not sure I can add value. What specifically do you expect me to be able to contribute?

When we created a training program for middle management on personal and leader effectiveness, we asked what caused employees the most frustration and wasted time.

The top two answers by a wide margin were too many emails and time-wasting meetings. I share here the secrets to holding effective meetings. You likely spend a significant part of your day attending meetings. Many of them will be unproductive.

Although meetings do not have to be a burden, changing your company's culture will take time. Start by setting a good example with the meetings you hold. If you are lucky, others will be so impressed that they will adopt your good habits for their own meetings.

10 Ways to Improve Your Meetings

1. Have an objective

Only schedule meetings when necessary. Don't have a meeting just because it's routine. Have a specific objective for every meeting. If you can't articulate a clear objective, you aren't ready for a meeting.

2. Use a goal-based agenda

Stick to a goal-based agenda for all meetings. Specify what you hope to achieve for each item on the agenda. Make a note of off-topic items raised during the meeting but don't let them derail the agenda.

3. Distribute material in advance

Meetings are more efficient if participants come prepared. Distribute the agenda and materials at least one day in advance and earlier if possible. Remember your colleagues all have other priorities.

4. Invite only necessary participants

Only invite participants who need to be there. You may decline meeting invitations if you will not add value. Ask the organizer to clarify your role if unclear.

5. Use cost-effective locations

Your meeting is not an excuse to travel to an exotic location. Unless the purpose of the meeting is pleasure, best to keep meetings and pleasure separate.

6. Use only time needed

Don't schedule 30- or 60-minute meetings just because that's what your calendar defaults to. Try scheduling 15- or 20-minute meetings instead.

Start meetings on time and end on time. If you accomplish your objectives early, end early.

7. Have proposals ready

Have proposals ready for decisions that need to be made at the meeting. Use the meeting time to discuss the proposals rather than the background so you can take action following the meeting.

8. Eliminate distractions and focus

Keep participants focused by asking them to put away phones and computers during the meeting — as needed, one person can take notes. Break every couple of hours to allow time for participants to respond to urgent calls.

9. Distribute notes and action items

Send notes and action items that come from the meeting promptly following the meeting.

These tips are powerful because people can implement them easily. You just have to want to do it and then be mindful of what you are doing. Thus, I will end with my final tip for holding effective meetings:

10. Don't send that invitation before reviewing your agenda and materials against this checklist

With practice, you will become skilled at making the most effective use of your colleagues' time. If you follow this checklist, you are much more likely to hold effective meetings that do not waste time.

But remember that the best meeting might be the one you never attended.

Be well.

Chapter Twenty

Persuade Like Aristotle

Part of the Master Skills series on how to crush your job with better communication — five ideas on the path to persuasion

If you want to know which students will become successful lawyers, it turns out the law school admissions test is not the best predictor. A few years ago professors Marjorie Schultz and Sheldon Zedeck identified 26 lawyer effectiveness factors that serve as better predictors of career success.

The whole list makes for interesting reading. Here I focus on one set of skills the professors grouped under the "Communications" heading:

- **Influencing and advocating**. Persuades others of position and wins support.

- **Writing**. Writes clearly, efficiently, and persuasively.

- **Speaking**. Orally communicates issues in an articulate matter consistent with the issue and audience being addressed.

- **Listening**. Accurately perceives what is being said both directly and subtly.

You can be well-liked, rigorous in your analysis, and correct in your conclusions. But inevitably, someone whose pay depends on disagreeing with you is going to challenge your views. It thus will come as no surprise to all of you working in the real world that being persuasive is pretty important.

With all this in mind, I was annoyed that no one told me the secret to effective persuasion is no secret at all. That, in fact, it has been known for over 2,000 years thanks to Aristotle's *Rhetoric*.

I spent the better part of 20 years watching, teasing out best practices, and honing my own skills at being the Gerry Spence of the boardroom.

Time-tested advice with modern tweaks

One of the things I learned is that no matter how strong your persuasion skills, you can get better. Although I bet you're already pretty good, today I will give you a condensed version of time-tested advice on how to persuade, together with a few modern tweaks.

I personally put the lessons here into practice every time I have to teach or present. Here are five elements Aristotle believed were critical to effective persuasion,* to which I will add a few observations:

1. Ethos (Credibility)

Ethos is that part of your talk where you give the audience insight as to why you are credible. This can come by virtue of your position or from your specific experience.

I find you build credibility by never lying or shading the truth, even when it hurts your case. Admitting a weakness upfront is a great way to show you can be trusted.

It also helps to be transparent about your interests. People know you are representing a position, so go ahead and tell them what you want.

2. Logos (Appeal to reason)

Having set the stage about your credentials as a person, this is where you use facts and data to form a rational argument.

Everyone likes to think they are logical, rational thinkers. So help them see a clear path to your point of view. Think of it as a fact-based hook for people to hang their hat on, something that allows them to agree with you.

3. Pathos (Human emotion)

Notwithstanding what we just said about the appeal to reason, the most powerful persuasion is carried on the wings of emotion.

And the single best vehicle for arousing emotions is the story. The bulk of your presentation therefore comes in the form of storytelling. This doesn't have to be a fully-fledged plotline. You do well to call upon a simple anecdote or episode from your life.

4. Be tangible

Particularly when you are trying to get your audience to accept or understand a new idea, analogies and metaphors are great tools. They give the impression that the new thing is really just something the audience already understands. And they make otherwise abstract ideas tangible and vivid.

5. Be concise

People have short attention spans, now more than ever. Don't fight it. Instead, make your argument short and simple. Start strong and end strong.

In the business context, I assume your audience knows you and knows why you are there. Don't waste time and valuable attention on introductions, background, or other unimportant topics.

I say jump right into the heart of your story and grab the audience's curiosity. Storytelling is so important to persuasion that I start with it always, even when I have to take pains to later build credibility and the logical argument.

Practice your prepared remarks enough so that you can speak fluidly. Speak written remarks out loud at least once, even if only to yourself. This will help you catch awkward phrases that don't sound right.

Be animated, speak with energy, and show interest and enthusiasm in your subject. Your excitement shines through to your listeners. But don't let your enthusiasm carry you away. Speak clearly and pace yourself. Get a friend to point out your "ums" and "ahs" and similar empty words.

Watch your audience carefully for clues as to how you're doing. Help them keep the thread of your story by stepping back on significant transitions:

This is where we are. I just discussed X, and now I am going to move on to Y.

I hope the law and the facts will always be on your side. When they are not, you need to be the best persuader in the room. And that is more a matter of preparation than anything else.

I hope today's discussion arms you well for the battles ahead.

Be well.

* I was inspired to take up the discussion of Aristotle's Rhetoric by the HBR article The Art of Persuasion Hasn't Changed in 2,000 Years.

Chapter Twenty-One

Listen Up Already!

Part of the Master Skills series on how to crush your job with better communication — active listening explained

When I teach law students about effective communication, I start by telling them the most important skill is none of what they're usually taught. It's not writing clearly or learning to be a great presenter. It is listening.

Teaching lawyers how to listen is surprisingly hard. It's hard because it seems trivial. Everyone in my classes thinks they already know how to do it. Ironic, isn't it, that the greatest barrier to learning how to listen is that people don't listen to the lesson?

For all the articles saying listening is important and giving advice about how to do it better, I find few digging into details about *why* listening is so important.

They'll say listening well builds trust, encourages openness, or shows respect. Listening does do these things but they're not the most important reason to listen well.

On a human level, we have a deep need to feel heard and be understood.

- Good listening builds a connection between you and the other person.

- That connection, in turn, allows both participants to engage in a conversation that tackles meaningful topics.

- We are far more likely to listen to someone whom we feel is listening to us.

That's why if you want to be a great communicator, you need to create connections by listening.

A good listener stands out

The great majority of modern interactions are superficial, fleeting, and of little consequence. In the work-from-home era, we're having fewer in-person conversations. Emails, social media, and Zoom calls punctuate our days.

Thus, when someone slows down and appears to be willing to take time for a deep conversation, it stands out.

The traditional advice for listening better is to practice what's called "**active listening**." First developed as a tool to help clinical psychologists be more effective counselors to their patients, active listening has become mainstream in the business context.

Unfortunately, the message got garbled in translation on the journey from psychology to business.

Active listening tips

I say this because there seems to be no consistent description of how to practice active listening. Most systems suggest listeners follow these steps:

- Pay careful attention, listening to verbal and non-verbal cues.

- Do not be judgmental or criticize what the person is saying, simply listen openly.

- Think about what you hear and seek to clarify your understanding.

- Repeat back what you heard and ask the person to confirm if it is correct.

Probably the biggest difference between active listening and what normally passes for conversation is the focus on the initial speaker.

As the listener, you do not seek to introduce any new thoughts or ideas until you have luxuriated in the first person's thoughts. Explore their topic, look at it from multiple angles, and make sure you have really given their thoughts proper air time.

You may never get to raise your own thoughts because, after all, this is about listening to the other person.

Contrast this with a normal conversation, which is you waiting for the other person to take a breath and stop blathering so you can get a word in edgewise.

Turns out, however, that the advice for clinical psychologists on listening to patients doesn't transfer perfectly to the business world.

Active listening in business

When we evaluate who is the most effective listener in the business context, we want something different:

- Paying attention does not mean silently listening. The best listeners ask constructive questions. This demonstrates that they are following along and understand what the speaker is saying.

- Withholding judgment is not enough. Effective listeners give positive feedback that encourages the speaker to be open. They do not necessarily agree with everything the speaker says, but nor are they trying to win a debate.

- A good listener also gives suggestions that make the conversation flow back and forth. They serve as a sounding board for the speaker's ideas and help develop and improve them.

I usually end these Master Skills articles by urging you to follow the checklist of steps I've outlined. I won't do that here. Indeed, my advice for you is not to get hung up about whether you're actively listening or exactly what steps to follow.

While I hope the tips above inspire you to try some new things out, a single step will make you stand out as a super-listener: simply paying attention and focusing on the other person without immediately trying to introduce your own point.

Because listening is becoming a lost art, people will notice when you really pay attention to them.

Be well.

Chapter Twenty-Two

What Lawyers Can Teach Us About Writing Well

Writing in plain language is a pleasure

Your readers love it when you write in plain language. Plain language means text they understand on the first reading.

Bryan Garner is a towering figure in the legal world. He's written many books on how to write persuasively and clearly. But his wise words are known mostly to lawyers.

I share the best of his plain English writing tips here. These are taken from his book *Legal Writing in Plain English*. I think you'll agree his tips can make us all better writers.

Framing your thoughts: The most productive hour

Have something to say — and think it through. Of all the things you might mention, what are the most important points? Practice leaving out everything that doesn't help you make your point.

Plan your writing projects in a four-step process, and keep the steps *separate*:

1. Brainstorm lots of things you want to say (10 minutes)

2. Outline a sensible order for those thoughts (5 minutes)

3. Using the outline, write a quick draft (25 minutes)

4. Edit your draft (10 minutes).

Organize your material

Order your material in a logical sequence and keep related material together. Divide your document into sections and use informative headings.

- Headings and subheadings help you organize your thoughts

- They make it easier for your readers to follow your argument

- They make your text skimmable

- They signal transitions

- They provide a road map when collected into a table of contents

Crafting sentences

Omit needless words. This enhances your clarity, makes readers faster, and gives your writing impact. You will struggle to write concisely at first. You can fix this in editing.

Keep your average sentence length to about 20 words. But also use variety, i.e. some longer and some shorter sentences.

Keep the subject, verb, and object together at the beginning of the sentence. This is how we think. When we read a sentence, we're looking for the action.

Prefer the active voice over the passive. If you're active, you do things. If you're passive, things are done to you. The active voice brings you several advantages:

1. It usually requires fewer words

2. It better reflects chronological sequences

3. It makes the reader's job easier

4. It makes your writing more vigorous and lively

End your sentences emphatically, with a kick. What you end with you emphasize. Choose wisely.

Choosing words

Root out jargon that you can simplify.

Use strong verbs. Minimize is, are, was, and were. Turn — ion words into verbs when you can.

Simplify wordy phrases. Watch out for "of." Can you kill half of them?

Make everything you write speakable. It's OK to use contractions. Readers like the sense that a writer is talking directly to them.

Be well.

Chapter Twenty-Three

What the Government Can Teach Us About Writing Well

Writing in plain language is a pleasure

Your readers love it when you write in plain language. Plain language means text they understand on the first reading. I summarize here the key points from the best government guidance on writing.

"Wait, did you say the *best government* guidance? I thought governments were terrible at communicating clearly." That's normally true, but they've been working hard to get better.

President Obama signed The Plain Writing Act of 2010. It requires U.S. federal agencies to communicate clearly in a way that the public can understand.

The government prepared guidelines to help agencies write better, and it is those guidelines that I summarize for you today. I think you'll agree they can make us all better writers.

Write for your audience

Writing for your audience means using language your audience understands and feels comfortable with. What is their current level of knowledge and expertise?

Put yourself in your reader's shoes and provide them with only what they need to know. What are they trying to accomplish? How does your writing help them? This includes anticipating what questions your reader will have.

Address the user: write as if you are speaking with one person. Use personal pronouns like "we" and "you." More than any other single technique, using personal pronouns like "you" pulls users into the information and makes it relevant to them.

Organize the information

Make your writing easy to follow. Organize material in a logical order.

- Put the most important information at the beginning. Include necessary background information towards the end.

- Similarly, put general information first, and specialized information or exceptions later.

- Consider likely questions.

Use a table of contents for longer documents. Add useful headings to guide the reader through your document. Make your headings descriptive and informative.

Lists make it easier to see all the steps in a process. Use a lead-in sentence to explain your list.

Choose your words carefully

Use simple words and phrases. Choose simple expressions over complicated ones.

- Avoid jargon and legalese.

- Minimize abbreviations and definitions.

- Avoid hidden verbs, which are verbs converted into nouns.

Be concise

Write short sentences and break up longer sentences into smaller units.

Keep the subject, verb, and object close together.

- Don't put modifiers between these parts.

- Put modifiers at the end of the sentence or in a new sentence.

Check your prepositions, such as "of," "on," and "to." They often mark phrases you can shorten.

Keep your writing conversational

Use the active voice. Specify who is performing the action.

Design for reading

Use an easy-to-read font, like Times New Roman.

Put your headings in bold text and use uppercase and lowercase letters, not all caps.

Use standard bullets, and not more than two types.

Highlight important concepts using **bold** and *italics.*

Use tables for complex material

Take a fresh look at your document when you are done.

- Is it easy to follow?

- Is it visually appealing?

Be well.

Chapter Twenty-Four

Two Editing Checklists May Save Your Story

Writing well is hard. Editing well is easy

Y our readers love it when you write in plain language. Plain language means text they understand on the first reading.

Here are simple editing tips originally developed for lawyers to write in plain language. You'll probably agree lawyers need the help. More importantly, these tips can help all of us write better.

Checklist of Basic Edits

1. Check punctuation, misused words, spelling, etc.

2. Convert the passive voice into the active voice

3. Use stronger verbs in place of "be" words (is, are, was, were, be, been)

4. Change words ending in — ion to verbs where you can

5. Check every "of" to see if can be rephrased to eliminate it

6. Try to cut each sentence by 25% or more

7. Read your work aloud. Does it read naturally?

If you want to advance to masterclass level, particularly for longer pieces with multiple points, apply these advanced editing tips.

Checklist of Advanced Edits

1. Have you achieved the tone you wanted?

2. Does your central point emerge clearly and quickly?

3. Is there a strong counterargument you haven't addressed?

4. Can you spot a bridge at the outset of each paragraph?

5. For each block quotation, have you supplied an informative lead-in?

6. Can you phrase your points more memorably? Should you use bullets instead?

7. Have you kept citations out of the main text? Doing so improves readability. You should always cite sources but use footnotes or endnotes instead.

Be well.

N.B. – Inspired by *Legal Writing in Plain English* by Bryan Garner.

Chapter Twenty-Five

Breaking News: Lawyer Settles Oxford Comma Debate

It's not a question of style or personal preference. A simple rule of thumb to avoid exposing yourself to needless risk

I f you have an opinion about the Oxford comma, let it be an informed opinion.

I am informed that people have been fighting about it since The University of Oxford was founded in the 12th century, a full three centuries before the comma itself was even invented.

More recently, I spent 25 years writing and reviewing SEC filings.

- When companies make a mistake in these public documents they face legal liability.

- Expensive lawyers like me thus spend hours checking every sentence to ensure companies' disclosures are clear.

- This work taught me more than I ever wanted about the Oxford comma.

Here's my simple rule of thumb about the Oxford comma that you are free to use yourself:

If you are a corporate lawyer writing SEC disclosure documents, use the Oxford comma or risk getting sued for malpractice.

What's the fuss about the Oxford comma?

Simply put, when you list three or more items in a sentence, people debate including a comma (the Oxford comma) before the last item. They argue it changes the style of your writing and the look of your sentence.

People who did not go to law school lose sleep worrying about all the ink needlessly spilled when using a comma in sentences where it may be plausibly omitted.

"Think of the children!" they cry.

Is there a difference between using it or not?

The truth about the Oxford comma is that it's much more than stylistic. That's because the comma serves a specific purpose. And the clauses mean very different things when you use the comma or omit it.

When a sentence is ambiguous or its meaning is disputed, judges apply simple rules of construction (i.e. interpretation) to resolve the dispute:

- When you include the comma, it means you are describing a list of three or more distinct items.

- When you do not include the comma, it means the final two items in the list are examples of the previous item on the list.

What if I'm not a corporate lawyer writing SEC documents?

I feel sorry for you. The next best thing is to imply to others that you do important stuff for a living.

How? You signal your importance to the cognoscenti by punctiliously using the Oxford comma.

If small-minded people challenge you, I recommend adopting a superior tone and explaining that there are at least two reasons to use the Oxford comma.

- First, you eliminate potential ambiguity when you include the comma. That alone is reason enough to use the comma and should satisfy most doubters.

- If the person insists on hearing your second reason, tell them this. In the large majority of cases, you are in fact describing a list of distinct items. Only rarely are you modifying the prior item in your list with examples.

True, you're probably not facing millions of dollars in legal exposure by skipping a comma. But can you really afford to take the risk?

Be well.

Chapter Twenty-Six

If You Scheduled Your Day Like an Airline

If you let your aim point downwards, even a little bit, don't be surprised if you end up in places you don't want to be

W ell, that didn't take long. No sooner are we back to business travel than the airlines remind us why flying is so maddening.

To illustrate, let's assume your boss has started scheduling meetings the way airlines schedule their flights. How would that look?

Boss's Assistant: *"Oh hi, Peony. I'm calling about your request for a meeting with Gorgon."*

You: *"Great, thank you, Agonia! We have a big decision coming up, and I need Gorgon's input. How does next week look?"*

"Ha, ha, ha! You're so cute. Let's see, I have some availability in three months' time."

"What, really? I need only a few minutes of Gorgon's time. Isn't there an earlier time available?"

Heavy sigh. *"Well, there is a slot in two weeks, but … ."*

"I'll take it. I really need to talk with Gorgon."

"I'll send you an invite. Bye Peony."

A few days before the meeting

"Hello Agonia. I'm calling about the meeting invite you sent for the 10th."

"Yes. Do you have the meeting reference number?"

"What? Er, it's the meeting with Gorgon starting at 3 pm on the 10th."

"I need the reference number. We categorize Gorgon's meetings by reference number. It's clearly listed in your meeting reservation."

"Oh, that's new, hold on, let me look ... Agonia?" Calling back *"Hi there, Agonia. We got disconnected somehow."*

"What can I do for you Peony?"

"I found the meeting number. It's C&xD*çRiuP."

"Sorry, I don't have any meeting scheduled with that number."

You, repeating number: *"Wait, is that a ?"*

"I have it. What can I help you with?"

"Well, I'm a little confused. It says here my meeting lasts for two hours. I only need 20 or 30 minutes at most."

"Gorgon is keen on making efficient use of employees' time. The last thing he wants is for you to be late for your next meeting. Best to stick with this schedule, because then you can be sure to finish on time."

"I guess so, but I'm not sure how that makes efficient use of my time. Anyway, never mind that. The meeting invite says I should come to Gorgon's office at 1 pm already. That's two hours before the meeting starts!"

"Yes, and be happy you're not visiting from one of the international offices. International employees have to come three hours before their meeting is scheduled to start."

"But why?!"

"Well, we also want to make efficient use of Gorgon's time. Once an employee came five minutes late to a meeting, and it threw off Gorgon's schedule for the whole

morning. We never wanted that to happen again, so now we require employees to come two hours early to make sure the meeting will start on time."

Muttering under your breath. *"What's this about checking my meeting readiness the day before the meeting?"*

"Gorgon just wants to make sure you're ready for the meeting. It helps if you send everything in advance, including your slides, the project charter, the names of the other executives involved, and the meeting minutes."

"But I don't have any of that! I just need to talk with Gorgon for a few minutes to get some input. He knows what this is about."

"If you'd like, I can reschedule the meeting for a later time when you'll be ready … ?"

"No, no! I guess I can send something in advance. Let's just leave it."

The day of the meeting

Arriving on the executive floor, you see a line of faces standing in the hallway outside Gorgon's office. You recognize two colleagues.

"Sade, Maddie! What are you doing here in the hallway?"

Maddie: *"Waiting for our meeting with Gorgon. Mine was scheduled for noon, but he's running behind again."*

Sade: *"Ours was yesterday afternoon, but that got cancelled. Technical problems or something."*

Recalling that you saw Gorgon leaving at 3 pm yesterday with golf clubs, you say: *"Oh, sorry to hear that. Who are all these other people? And why are you all in the hallway?"*

Maddie: *"Agonia only lets us in at the time our meeting starts. We used to be able to wait in her office, but once someone talked too loudly on their cell phone, so now we only get to go in once our meeting is called."*

"Gosh, it's not so comfortable out here. I'll just sit on the floor over here and try to get some work done."

Two hours later

"Peony? Time for your meeting."

You, getting to your feet and whispering to yourself, *"Finally!"*

"Come on in. We pride ourselves in making sure Gorgon's meetings start on time. Take a seat along this wall. We put in an extension cord so you can charge your laptop while you wait. Not sure it's working after someone spilled water on it, but it's the thought that counts, right?"

You, noticing that most of the people who were waiting in the hallway are now waiting in Agonia's office. *"Agonia, I thought my meeting was starting."*

"Your meeting did start, dear. It's just that you won't see Gorgon for a little while yet because of congestion from earlier meetings. I'll give you an update on the schedule as soon as I know more."

You, thinking to yourself, *"I'm so glad I brought my power bank today."*

Two further hours go by. It is now a little after 5 pm.

"Peony, Gorgon will see you now, quickly, hurry."

You, grabbing your things and rushing into Gorgon's office. *"Gorgon, hi. I'll keep this brief. I put everything you asked for in the slides and summary memo. I recommend we go with Option A, although Option B would cost us 10 percent less."*

Gorgon, looking blank. *"I don't think I saw your summary. Maybe you can send it by email, and also drop off a hard copy with Agonia. I've been really busy."*

You, looking at Gorgon's spotless desk and empty office, are at a loss for words.

"Anyway, I'm running a bit behind today, so if there's nothing else … ."

Agonia enters. *"Come along Peony. Look at that will you, we started on time and finished on time, as promised! We are keeping up our perfect track record."*

You, unable to help yourself, *"Agonia, I got here two hours early, waited in your office for two more hours, and now we finished 15 minutes late. How is that on time?"*

"Well Gorgon is so busy, we agreed with the CEO that any meeting that starts and ends within 15 minutes of its scheduled time will count as an on-time meeting. Isn't that wonderful!"

"What? Wait, why are we going out this back door to the fire escape? I left my coat in your office."

"Oh, just come by again tomorrow to pick it up. We found that it was confusing to have people coming and going from the same door, so now we have departing attendees leave this way."

"But security only lets people onto the executive floor if they have a scheduled meeting! I need my coat."

"Your meeting invite did say to keep your belongings with you at all times, Peony. But don't worry, schedule another meeting and I'm sure everything will be fine."

People can get used to almost anything if it is presented in small steps. It is only by looking back at the cumulative effect of many small changes that we realize how far we've come.

We often don't realize how many aspects of our lives are affected by this. Prices raised a few percent at a time, the amount included in a package shrunk ever so slightly, and online terms are just a bit less favorable with each revision.

If you let your aim point downwards, even a little bit, don't be surprised if you end up in places you don't want to be.

This is the flip side of continuous improvement, where small positive changes made steadily over time lead to impressive results. Let's call it dissolution by degree.

Pay attention to what you accept in your performance.

It may be too late for airlines, but it's not too late for us as we manage our careers.

Be well.

Chapter Twenty-Seven

How to Spot a Bad Lawyer

The rule of law must benefit everyone equally or it is meaningless. And the time for us to be especially wary is when we feel most strongly about a cause

T he comedians among the public are itching to answer something like: "Did they graduate from a law school?" Or: "Are they admitted to practice law?" Lawyer jokes are rampant because lawyers, sadly, live up to and exceed the public's worst expectations of us.

I'm thinking beyond sleazy personal injury lawyers and slithery prosecutors. I will explore with you here how we feel at heart about one of the hardest legal duties: Staying objective in difficult circumstances and upholding the rule of law.

The law is supposed to apply equally to us all

We learn in school about the rule of law and how preserving it is vital to maintaining a democratic society. We tell ourselves we operate in nations of laws, not nations of individuals, where laws apply equally to all.

So what is a lawyer to do when the facts point one way and the law another, when our potential client is truly odious, or when our personal beliefs go against what the law dictates? The answer is clear, at least for a law student, but in practice, lawyers' behavior is anything but.

Let's take a few examples to illustrate.

Let's say you work for a famous civil rights organization, dedicated to defending free speech. Does it matter whether you only take cases from people whose speech you agree with?

- In the era of Trump-inspired lies, what if you refused to defend someone's right to free speech specifically because you disagreed with their viewpoints? Well, you wouldn't be much of a defender of free speech, would you? That's precisely the position the ACLU finds itself in today.

Now consider Harvey Weinstein, a deeply unsympathetic person. Accused of forcing himself on a string of vulnerable women, he is what comes to mind under the definition of "odious client." But does a client's unpopularity justify refusing him a defense? In today's charged atmosphere, many otherwise serious people think it does.

- Harvard University law professor Ronald Sullivan came under intense criticism for agreeing to serve on Weinstein's defense team, with Harvard firing him as faculty dean of an undergraduate house. (Sullivan ultimately withdrew from the defense team.)

- One commentator at the time wrote, "The reason we think of civil rights lawyers as doing 'good work' is because they chose just causes." (Nathan J. Robinson, Lawyers are Responsible for their Choice of Clients)

Nothing could be more wrong. In its heyday, the ACLU defended the KKK and was proud to defend pornographers. The good work is defending the rule of law, not whatever cause happens to have majority approval at that moment in time.

Now imagine you are a judge.

- If plaintiffs' and defendants' lawyers get carried away at times, we can chalk it up to our desire to be zealous advocates for our clients.

- The judge has no such excuse or expectation. Among all lawyers, we expect judges to be the most impartial, literally and figuratively above it all. At its most fundamental level, our courts determine the very validity of our laws.

What happens when judges take it personally?

What then would you say about a judge who decides a case because she identifies with one side more than the other, or has strong personal feelings about the morality and not legality of conduct?

What would you say about a judge who can be counted to vote in line with their racial or gender preferences, or their political affiliation, no matter the law? These are all easy questions.

- The lawyer who defends only free speech for those he agrees with?

- The lawyer who refuses any objectionable clients?

- The judge who decides cases by personal feeling and party affiliation?

Bad lawyers all. Bad because they undermine the rule of law for nothing more than fickle emotion and public sentiment.

I had these thoughts when seeing the uproar over the leaked US Supreme Court draft opinion overturning *Roe vs. Wade*. By the way, the leaker themselves: Bad lawyer, for the same reason that they undermine the rule of law.

Is the benefit of putting pressure on a Supreme Court justice in any case worth undermining the legitimacy of the entire court?

Be careful what you expect of your lawyer

What does it say about us and the rule of law that we think it matters who nominates our Supreme Court justices or what their political affiliation might be? Or that their skin color, gender, or ethnic background, is even part of the discussion?

Bad lawyers these days are sadly easy to spot. Let's make an effort not to join their ranks.

The way to do this is to remember the rule of law must benefit everyone equally or it is meaningless. And the time for us to be especially wary is when we feel most strongly about a cause.

Be well.

Chapter Twenty-Eight

How In-house Counsel Reinforce the Rule of Law

We must support freedom of expression, which includes dissenting opinions

In-house counsel are quick to agree to the principle that all people and institutions should be subject to laws that are fairly administered. We are vital links in defending the rule of law because it falls to us to adopt policies and enforce them fairly.

In practice, this means that we must apply the rules equally to everyone, regardless of their performance or position in the company. It means we respect employees' fundamental rights, including the right to privacy, freedom of expression, and due process.

Throughout history individuals worried most about intrusion by governments because they held asymmetrical power over citizens. Today, corporations play a much greater role in enhancing, or weakening, the rule of law.

Consider the following examples. As a condition to selling their product in a local market, a company may be asked to:

- Provide a version of their product that gives a government back-door access rights to private communications in their country.

- Allow governments to prevent certain groups from using the platform at all, or from discussing certain topics on the platform.

- Comply with government requests to censor disfavored individuals and limit the spread of their ideas.

A company's own employees may also create pressure on management and in-house counsel. For example, employees may demand the company cease doing legal business with disfavored customers. Employees may expect the CEO to make a public statement on controversial topics, which is guaranteed to alienate potential customers either way.

What's our fiduciary duty as in-house counsel when our companies come under government pressure or employee pressure?

Censorship and cancellation requests

Here I'll focus on just one particularly harmful practice: Requests to suppress disfavored speech and to promote only consensus narratives. Whether on controversial topics or from controversial actors, how should in-house counsel respond to censorship or cancellation requests?

Giving in to these requests can seem like the path of least resistance. When we consider the effect our actions have on the rule of law, however, our choice becomes clearer: We must support freedom of expression, which includes dissenting opinions.

Here is a pledge you can commit to in defending freedom of expression within your company. If you follow these steps, you will be leading by example.

From this point forward, we will:

- Only say things in public and in private that we believe to be true, and will resist speech being forced upon us by protestors, employees, or the government;

- Not support isolated examples of someone's speech or thoughts can be used as an excuse to silence a person whose ideas challenge the orthodoxy; and

- Not participate in any training, lecture, or speech where the speaker promotes policies that divide us on the basis of immutable characteristics like skin color.

This is just a partial list of ways for you to reinforce freedom of expression. If you start to follow these habits, you will no doubt apply them well in additional settings.

Your resistance will be met with resistance, and some will fall prey to the ravages of the mob and be canceled. **There is no exception to upholding the rule of law.**

Hold fast to the rule of law

No matter your position, no matter your political leaning, no matter your past support, you will be confronted with the choice to give in to cancellation requests. Your decision shapes your character each time and helps set your company's fate.

Even this simple step of holding fast to the rule of law is hard if you have become used to going along to get along. But holding fast is not as hard as the alternative that awaits if we give in too often.

Holding fast to the rule of law is not an easy path, but it is the least difficult of all other alternatives. Already today there are those demonstrating what it means to stick to their principles. Join your voices to theirs and neither of you stands alone!

The more people that embrace the evenhanded application of the rule of law, the quicker we will put an end to the tyranny of the cancellers. If we are not one or two, but hundreds or thousands, their power will evaporate.

Be well.

Chapter Twenty-Nine

When the Best Course of Action is Inaction

By spending precious resources to improperly or only partially deal with problems, we can easily make things worse

H ave you noticed there is an incredible bias toward action at work? Just consider what happens when we identify a problem. The single correct response is to craft a solution. We are so motivated to do something, anything, that we overlook one of nature's great problem-solvers: Doing nothing.

This is no paean to procrastination for the sake of being lazy. No, let me tell you why our desire to intervene, to meddle, and to change things is so often counterproductive. In brief, it's because crafting effective solutions to real problems is hard. By spending precious resources to improperly or only partially deal with problems, we can easily make things worse.

Our desire to tackle problems is admirable. We should celebrate the mindset that says "We can do this," and does not shy away from hard work. But let us not mistake good intentions for good outcomes. Just because we have our hearts in the right place, we get no free pass from accountability for results.

Practical and pragmatic

I had these thoughts after writing an article about how often government spending to achieve societal outcomes not only fails to achieve the desired outcome but rather worsens the very situation politicians want to improve.

Although the desirability of the policy objective cannot justify failed policies, it is depressing how often we hear only about the goals and never about the results.

Now to be fair, I thought it would be appropriate to shine the spotlight instead on corporations. How well do we do in solving the problems we set out to tackle? I admit I'm biased when I say that I believe corporations are pretty good at solving problems, at least compared to governments.

One key reason for better business performance is that we have skin in the game. That is, we're spending our own money, and we can't print more when we need it. This means we are more attuned to prioritizing solutions that may be practical and pragmatic, and much more wary of waste.

Pausing and problem-solving

But that's not to say companies are perfect at solving problems, are we? I explained several reasons why employees in corporations also fail to solve problems well in the earlier chapters Identifying Problems Worth Working On and Identifying Solutions That Will Work.

I recommend you have another look at these chapters before we get too confident about our problem-solving abilities.

- In short, we are distracted by pressing but non-strategic problems, which means we waste our time.

- And we underestimate how hard it is to implement good solutions by failing to account for the full costs our solution requires and the world's stubborn resistance to change.

Now let's consider what happens when we pause instead of jumping immediately into implementing solutions. The pause gives us precious time to spend thinking about our problem.

By considering my earlier advice about how to both choose problems worth solving and design solutions most likely to succeed, we increase the odds we can craft a better solution than if we jumped in with well-meant but misguided action.

And here's something else to keep in mind about waiting. When you wait you will be amazed how often your problem turns into something different than it first appeared. Sometimes what looked like a massive problem turns out to be just a few anecdotes that got blown out of proportion.

Because humans are such great pattern-recognition machines, we see connections where none exist. My favorite problems were the ones that simply evaporated when we left them alone. This happened often.

Sitting with the problem

Or maybe you realize upon reflection that what looked like the root cause of the problem isn't the only cause or even the main one. Difficult problems typically have multiple causes, and focusing too quickly on one increases the likelihood your solution will be partially effective at best.

When you give yourself time to sit with a problem, you can spend some time thinking about the foreseeable but unintended consequences of any proposed actions. Is what you want to do entirely consistent with your company's values? Could someone seeing only part of the problem or part of the solution reasonably misunderstand or criticize your actions?

The pause also provides you time to conduct a pre-mortem, in which you forecast the future and brainstorm all the ways your solution could fail to address the problem. Anticipating why your solution may fail is so helpful to good problem-solving that you should never embark on a costly solution without first wallowing in its likely failure.

For all these reasons, I say the next time you're facing a problem at work, take a deep breath and ... do nothing, at least for a while.

And if anyone asks why you're not doing something, tell them you're doing the hardest thing: thinking.

Be well.

Chapter Thirty

If We Are What We Eat, Be Worried

We seem indifferent to the impact of the ideas we consume because we assume we can control what we think

Most people believe they are directly affected by the food they eat. Hence the successive panics resulting in regulating various components of and micronutrients in food: salt, fat, sugar, lactose, gluten, genetically modified organisms (GMOs), hormones, and much more.

It's as if we assume our body is just a physical machine, and so the food we put into our body is going to have a clear impact on how the machine works. It's just chemistry!

In contrast, people act as if their mental processes have a master governor overseeing everything in the form of our minds or consciousness. As a result, we seem indifferent to the impact of the ideas we consume because we assume we can control what we think.

Consider how badly nutrition science has performed in understanding how our bodies operate — mere machines.

- The consuming public suffered repeated gross errors from scientists underestimating the body's complexity.

- By focusing on just a small piece in a carefully controlled lab environment, they thought they could explain the whole system and failed badly.

Is it possible we have similarly underestimated the mind's complexity?

Maybe there's more going on in our heads than the conductor in our consciousness we imagine is carefully and logically orchestrating our lives. Why is the prevalence of mental illness among adults higher than it's ever been? Why are more children depressed than ever before?

Can we say anything about how the mind works and how people come to form their ideas? In some ways, psychology has been much more successful than nutrition. If we still cannot say exactly what we should eat to maintain a healthy weight, we have learned a lot about how to influence and manipulate people.

We're affected by propaganda

The science of propaganda has a long and dark history, but that's because it works and repeatedly has been put to nefarious purposes. Here's an excerpt from a foundational 1930 text:

> ... *Propaganda means an effort deliberately to manufacture popular opinions and attitudes and thus to control popular conduct; and usually the implication is that the aims of the propagandists are concealed. The objects of propaganda do not know the purposes of the makers of the propaganda. Propaganda then is the propagation of ideas, opinions and attitudes, the real purpose of which is not made clear to the hearer or reader.* – Social Psychology: An Analysis of Social Behavior, Kimball Young

I've been thinking recently about the prevalence of propaganda in the West. We are by no means exempt from people trying to deliberately manufacture popular opinions and attitudes. In some ways, because of our democratic systems, we are even more routinely subject to such campaigns.

Our politicians gain power in part by detecting the winds of popular opinion and then riding along, but also in part by seeking to shape popular opinion in ways they think will be to their advantage.

Every time you hear a complex topic reduced to a catchy slogan you are being propagandized. It happens to us so frequently that we scarcely notice.

Look at how any significant legislation is described by both sides in a debate. You will see almost no substantive discussion of the actual law because laws are complex and it takes time to discuss them accurately. Instead, you see a scramble to label the law with a slogan that the media will then repeat.

When smart, educated people ignore facts

Since I retired, I've been traveling around and meeting with people across the country. I'll tell you what's both shocked and frightened me. Not that people have different ideas and beliefs on hot-button topics. That's to be expected.

It's rather that people I know to be smart and assumed to be well-informed had obvious and serious gaps in their basic information. They held opinions in good faith but were acting without all the facts.

I don't want to give specific examples of my conversations, because I would send a number of you into cognitive dissonance. That is, you'd say, "I never heard of that. What's James talking about? I know my sources are good. He must be crazy." And you'd dismiss my whole argument as flawed.

It's easy, though, for you to recall times when someone — a clueless someone — disagreed with you on a basic point. They were so obviously wrong: They either ignored facts or simply didn't know fundamental things. That's what I'm talking about.

How much can we control what we think?

Come back now to your faith in the idea that you have a mental governor (or mind or consciousness) that regulates how you think about the world.

You can consume any media and make up your own mind about what your values and beliefs are, right? Well, if that's so, how do you explain the wide disparity in what your fellow citizens believe? Surely you don't think their minds work fundamentally differently than yours.

Not to stretch the analogy, but there is every reason to believe modern media is feeding us a diet of junk food. Blatant propaganda that, because we're force-fed it, we come to accept.

- Much of what we think we know is wrong.

- People are missing vital nutrients from their diet of information and ideas.

- As a result, we don't know what we don't know.

Is there any solution to this problem? I am not sure. My advice is to keep an open mind to the idea that you may be misinformed. Be less sure about what you think you know.

Allow for the possibility that you cannot so easily control what you think and that you may be influenced by what you consume. That chances are good none of our media is impartial, even though I know you think yours is.

If we are being propagandized, even a little, remember that consuming poison is never going to make us healthy.

Be well.

Chapter Thirty-One

How Being Humble Can Help You Be Wrong Less Often

A person can be smart, well-intentioned, and sincere while also being dangerously wrong

L et me teach you how to disagree with yourself. That is, if you want to improve the quality of your thinking and decision-making. One way to do so is to regularly challenge your thinking.

I assume no one wants to fail at what they set out to do. I also understand that few people like to be reminded of their failures. But, if by studying our failures we can improve our odds of future success, I say the study is well worth the discomfort.

Even better, when we get into the habit of considering what could go wrong before we act, we can improve our odds of future success without having to first personally experience failure. In this chapter, I explore how being humble can lead us to make better decisions.

Shooting from the hip is for the foolhardy

Johnny Mercer wrote the lyrics in 1940 to what could be the unofficial decision-maker's anthem: Fools Rush In (Where Angels Fear to Tread).

But I prefer the earlier formulation by Alexander Pope in An Essay on Criticism:

Foolish people are often reckless, attempting feats that the wise avoid.

(N.B. This could also serve as the rallying cry for every technical writer preparing warning labels for consumer goods products.)

While avoiding reckless behavior is a worthy goal, inaction is no answer. To make progress in business, relationships, and life, we must act.

I recall our CEO frequently exhorting us to have a "bias for action." Analyze as necessary, but make sure not to be paralyzed by wanting to perfect your analysis. Sooner than you feel ready, plan to take concrete action. Even if the original plan is not perfect, we can also make corrections while we're implementing it.

The ideal mix of analysis and action comes about when we plan to increase our odds of success while simultaneously contemplating how our plans could be frustrated. That is, identifying what are the things that could go wrong and derail us.

Planning for success while also contemplating failure is not intuitive, and most people can't do it reliably. In my experience, we like to focus on the pleasant daydreams of success rather than the ways we might flop.

Daydreaming of success is necessary and healthy, to a point. Taken too far, we risk falling into cognitive dissonance.

We fall in love with our plan and see all the ways that it will be great. But then we tend to filter new information to fit our view of the world. We easily disregard contrary indications and ignore warning signs.

We have two potential countermeasures to this blindness:

1. Conduct a pre-mortem

When working alone, we can ensure our personal project plans include a "pre-mortem" step. It's usually helpful to do this sometime after starting your planning, but before you get too near the end. Say halfway through your planning as a good rule of thumb.

The purpose of the pre-mortem is to daydream again, but this time you imagine all the ways your project could be frustrated. Nothing goes according to plan. Why is that?

Be broad in spinning out your disaster scenarios and try to come up with a lengthy list. Only once you've prepared a good list, rank your future obstacles in terms of likelihood, magnitude, and addressability.

- Focus some of your planning attention on more likely risks of consequence that you can pragmatically do something about.

- Ignore small risks, unlikely risks, and risks that you cannot reasonably plan around.

- But be creative in considering potential mitigation before dismissing a risk as too hard to plan around. Even if you can't think of a solution, if the risk is real and not unlikely, you might get some advice from others before moving on.

2. Make sure to invite a spoiler to the team

Our second countermeasure is available when we are working in teams: Assign a person specifically to think of the various spoiler scenarios while the rest of the team does its work.

When the spoiler has a good list, bring the team together for a brainstorming session. This serves to review and expand the list and then discuss possible countermeasures.

The benefits of the pre-mortem review go beyond identifying weaknesses and improving your plan. A good pre-mortem includes asking *"How will we know* if things are starting to go badly? What types of information will we collect, and who will review it?" This helps shield you from ignoring negative data after you've started to implement your plan.

We improve our vision by remembering our fallibility

We humans value the things we invest time and effort into. The harder you and your team work on a project, the more difficult it is for you to objectively identify and assess warning signs.

Knowing this, you can get help from people who are close to, but not directly involved in, your project. Have them monitor the data and assess for you whether you are on track or need to correct course.

A person can be smart, well-intentioned, and sincere while also being dangerously wrong. Relying on your good intentions to confirm the validity of your actions is risky indeed.

One way to improve our chances of being wrong less often is to be humbler.

When planning our initiatives and implementing them, use the pre-mortem process to identify how our plans might go awry. This includes designing processes for collecting good data, objectively reviewing that data, and adjusting course if results aren't coming in as hoped.

Doing so is no guarantee against being a fool rushing in, attempting feats the wise avoid, but it will make you more effective than most.

Be well.

Chapter Thirty-Two

Disagree Without Being Disagreeable

Ideas spread and become influential because they win over new adherents. If you want your ideas to gain traction you must expose them to people who do not yet agree with you

B ecause I believe continuous improvement principles can aid us in many areas, I am always looking for opportunities to do better. A good indication for such an opportunity is when I've had a setback or failure. My natural instinct is now to say, "Well, that sucked. How can I do better next time?"

Treating a painful experience as an opportunity for learning is useful for multiple reasons. It helps you get over the sting of disappointment, because you hope to learn something new. It keeps you focused on the future and away from dwelling on past mistakes. And you often do learn how to perform better, which helps you get better over time.

This is by way of introducing a change I've noticed in how people interact: People are emotional train wrecks, and many don't know how to have a civil discussion. When it comes to any topic people feel strongly about, rational and reasoned discussion is rare. Emotions drive the rules of engagement and emotions often carry the day.

Why is this hard for me? After all, I know from my psychology studies that humans are ruled more by emotions than reason, and that we all justify our emotional decisions with supposed reasons after the fact. I think it's due to my further education in law and business, and then a couple decades working as a business lawyer. This made me a rationalist to the core.

That means I like to discuss and agree on premises, apply logical reasoning, and explore reasonable conclusions, of which there may be more than one. There are almost always pros and cons, and costs and tradeoffs associated with every proposed solution.

Being a rationalist also means I often change my mind. Maybe I learn new facts, or the other person raises an argument I hadn't considered. Sometimes I take the opposite side of an argument just to make sure I understand it correctly. I try to be only weakly committed to my starting position.

This process worked well not just with like-minded business colleagues, but also with negotiation partners and opposing counsel. It was rare for someone to take a business discussion intensely personally, or to view an exploratory sally as anything other than a discussion.

Thus, I am still struggling with the fact that, increasingly, reasoned discussion is no way to win an argument, and introducing nuance is like bringing a skunk to a garden party. No one wants to see it, and if you try to stick it under their nose they shy away.

If my habitual method of expounding logical positions is ill-suited to discussing issues, I can tell you another method that doesn't work well: What everyone else is doing, namely giving free run to emotions and shouting at each other. Let me explain why, looking at both in-person interactions and those occurring remotely on-line.

In-person interactions appear more civil, and I think they are more civil. This is partly because social conventions still prevent a certain amount of direct hostility. But only in small part. My observation is that face-to-face conversations are more civil primarily because most people avoid controversial topics.

The first few minutes' conversation with a new person represents a kind of exploratory dance. Can I discern from this person's statements whether they are a (fill-in the blank for your appropriate measure): Progressive menace, liberal idiot, ultra-MAGA Trump supporter, hard-right conspiracy theorist, semi-fascist, etc. If you detect enemy sentiments, the conversation usually turns to safer, bland, and non-controversial topics. If, however, you hear sentiments similar to your own, you can spend time agreeing with each other and laughing at how clueless supporters of the other party are.

Contrast this with on-line interactions. Although many posts are superficial and unobjectionable, whenever a substantive topic is introduced, there is no tentative probing. The initial volley is more likely to be inflammatory, because people are usually trying to make a point. Also, there's no one to check your inner dialogue, where your every thought is positively genius. Of course, you're right!

The return volleys to your post are either (a) wholly in agreement, confirming your brilliance, or (b) from someone who is apparently attacking everything you stand for and your inherent worth as a person. The proper response to such a challenge is to counterattack. By not immediately agreeing with you, your commenter deserves to be punished, ridiculed, misquoted. Whatever serves to get them to apologize, acquiesce, or go away, and right quick.

When did we get so fragile? Since when does a question or a comment, indeed anything other than slavish agreement, represent an attack on our personal integrity? It could be because the primary purpose of social networks is not to engage in reasoned debate, but to identify like-minded persons.

My mistake seems to be in assuming that people who post ideas are open to discussing those ideas. Rather, people behave as if all they want is reinforcement or silence. In my old world of legal wrangling, silence can be taken as assent. This makes it hard for me to scroll by glaring logical errors. Or even to resist adding another perspective to a topic. Hey, do you think this could lead to unintended consequences? Or, I agree the societal objective is valid, but are there better ways to achieve the desired outcome?

Remember that ideas spread and become influential because they win over new adherents. If you want your ideas to gain traction you must expose them to people who do not yet agree with you. How should you deal with their questions and overcome potential objections?

Here's a tip that is supported by all my learnings in psychology, economics, law, and business: Personal insults are remarkably poor persuaders. Insults in an exchange signal failure, not that you're winning.

When I see someone resort to personal insults, I take it to mean their idea cannot withstand criticism. Moreover, you are all but guaranteeing that your counterpart will dismiss what you have to say further. This makes it that much harder to achieve a common understanding.

Disagreement does not have to be disagreeable. When you make an exchange personal, you not only lose the argument, you lose the chance to gain a convert to your idea.

If you find yourself shouting at strangers, stop and ask yourself why. It's unlikely to be changing anyone's mind. And I bet you don't feel better after doing it. If your method is ineffective, and makes you bitter and unhappy to boot, why are you still using it?

I don't expect everyone to be Spock-like in their reasoning. But I'd be happy to see reasonable minds disagree reasonably more often.

Be well.

Chapter Thirty-Three

The World's Worst Persuasion Tactic: Insults

If you're tired of political insults, take the no-insult pledge with me

President Trump is a giant bully and an ass for insulting his opponents. His violation of norms shocked the world and pushed a great many people into horrified opposition.

What's baffling is how ready his opponents are to resort to the precise tactics they deplore. (*We must destroy democracy to save democracy*.) The last decade presents a truly depressing spectacle to see who can most comprehensively violate norms.

To pick just a simple example, let's look at name-calling. It's more dangerous than we might think. Because of this, I make a personal commitment below and invite you to do the same.

It's one thing to disagree with a person and everything they stand for. It's another to spend hours of one's life dreaming up pejorative names.

When we resort to insults, we've already lost the argument

I've spent years learning how people think and how to get them to change their minds. My favorite lenses for understanding people and what motivates them have been psychology, economics, and law.

As General Counsel of a large public company for 20 years, I put these tools to good use in negotiating many thousands of contracts and deals with people all over the world. What they taught me is this: Personal insults are remarkably poor persuaders. Insults in an exchange signal failure, not that you're winning.

I wrote about this in Disagree Without Being Disagreeable:

> *When I see someone resort to personal insults, I take it to mean their idea cannot withstand criticism. Moreover, you are all but guaranteeing that your counterpart will dismiss what you have to say further. This makes it that much harder to achieve a common understanding.*

> *Disagreement does not have to be disagreeable. When you make an exchange personal, you not only lose the argument, you lose the chance to gain a convert to your idea.*

> *If you find yourself shouting at strangers, stop and ask yourself why. It's unlikely to be changing anyone's mind.*

If insults win no arguments, why do we hurl them at each other?

Here's where things get scary. Insulting an opponent (say, a politician) or a group (like their supporters) is not meant to change anyone's mind but to bolster opposition. That is, I want you to feel both righteous anger and a vicarious thrill when I insult our common enemy.

In other words, these insults are tools to divide citizens and dehumanize our enemies.

Reading history, I used to wonder how it is that so many seemingly enlightened and civilized societies found themselves turning on each other. How is it that neighbors could not only willingly, but happily, round up neighbors to imprison, torture, and even kill them?

I wonder no more. It starts with ceasing civil discussion in favor of bullying, shouting, and insulting. It's no joke, even if we find ourselves laughing.

The way to stop insulting people we disagree with...

I'll paraphrase Chief Justice John Roberts: The way to stop insulting people we disagree with is to stop insulting people we disagree with.

I will take the first step. Although I disagree with many people on politics, I hereby commit to the following no-insult pledge:

- I will never insult you personally for your political beliefs

- I will not personally insult a political figure I disagree with

- I will not become that which I despise to defeat that which I despise

- I will engage respectfully and in good faith, even when my political opponents do not

Fellow citizens, it's up to us. If our leaders won't serve as role models, let us do so ourselves. Take the no-insult pledge with me.

Be well.

Chapter Thirty-Four

How Not to Be a Sloppy Second Guesser

A short explanation of how risk management actually works

J oin me on a simple thought experiment to understand how risk management works. You can then apply these principles to your own life to make better decisions.

The umbrella decision

Let's imagine you're heading out for a walk. How do you decide whether to take an umbrella with you? Under what circumstances would you second-guess your decision?

How you feel about your decision depends on two things: What you knew before you left the house, and what happened outside until your feet once again cross the threshold of your door.

If it's a sunny day with a clear forecast, you have no trouble leaving the umbrella at home. The idea of taking it never crosses your mind.

Similarly, if it's already pouring out your decision is easy. We call it a no-brainer because you don't have to think.

Seen this way, it's clear all the magic happens amidst uncertainty. It's not raining now but it *might* rain later. You make a judgment call in the face of not knowing whether you'll need the umbrella or not.

Amidst uncertainty, we emphasize the downside

Let's say you decide to take the umbrella. Then if it rains, you feel good about your decision. You decided correctly!

- And if it doesn't rain, you are happy not to have needed your umbrella.

- You took reasonable action to mitigate a risk that didn't occur. You feel OK about it even though it was, in one sense, a "wasted" effort.

Now let's say you decide to take your chances and leave the umbrella at home. If it rains, you feel bad about your decision.

- To save yourself a small inconvenience (carrying the umbrella), your clothes were soggy all afternoon.

- But if it doesn't rain, you don't celebrate too much because you don't take an umbrella every day it doesn't rain.

When you mitigate risks, you are happy if they occur and fine if they don't occur. Remember you didn't know what would happen. It was a risk, not a certainty.

Second-guessing based on outcomes is common ... and wrong

The whole point of risk management is making decisions when the outcome is uncertain.

Thus, we properly judge such decisions based on the conditions when they were made, not on the ultimate outcome.

After events have played out, it is worse than useless to say "Knowing what we know now, you should have done X, not Y."

People do this all the time, however. Worse, they fall prey to hindsight bias and falsely remember what they thought and knew at the time.

Hindsight bias is widespread

You will hear people saying things like the following:

- "I could see the housing crisis forming. Anyone with half a brain knew the market was unsustainable."

- "Well, it's obvious that all that money printing and deficit spending was going to cause inflation."

- "I knew the vaccine wouldn't work. It was developed and rolled out in record time. It was a no-brainer not to put that unknown substance into my body."

To the sloppy second-guesser, taking steps to mitigate risks that occur is no big deal because the risk was obvious (in hindsight). And it was a wasted effort to mitigate risks that did not occur.

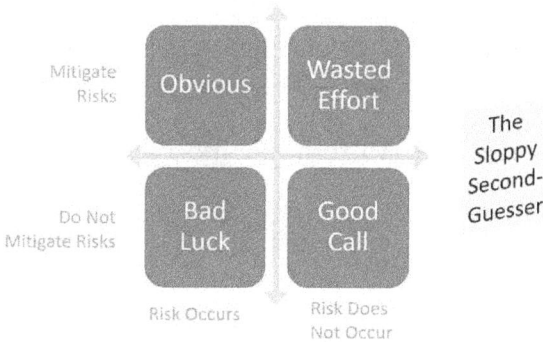

The sloppy second-guesser

Similarly, the sloppy second guesser thinks they made a good call when a risk they did nothing to mitigate does not occur and suffered from bad luck when it does.

It is no mistake to plan for risks that do not occur

Just as it is no mistake to plan for risks that never happen, it is no victory to hope for the best and get lucky. At least not from a risk management perspective.

The proper way to think about risk management under conditions of uncertainty is as follows:

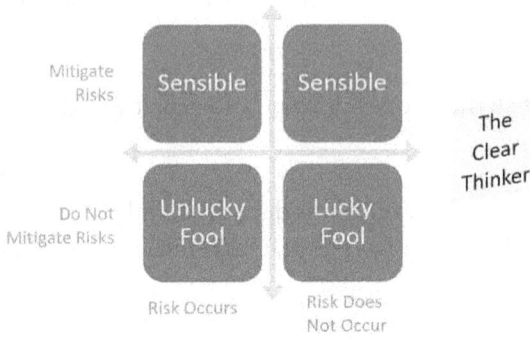

The clear thinker

It is sensible to mitigate against risk amidst uncertainty regardless of whether the risk occurs or not.

As a corollary, you are a fool not to mitigate risks, also regardless of outcomes. You are unlucky if the risk does not occur, and lucky if it does, but a fool either way.

Don't let what everyone knows after the fact turn you into a sloppy second guesser.

Be well.

Chapter Thirty-Five

I Think, Therefore, You're Wrong

If you disagree with something I've written the odds are quite good that I'm right. While I came to my approach accidentally, you can do it purposefully

I'm more likely to be right, not because I'm unusually smart, although that's part of it. It's rather because of another quirk in my personality. I'll start with the role of intelligence before turning to the quirk that makes me right annoyingly often.

You can use my method to be right more often, but it probably won't come naturally.

Smart people work best with other smart people

Oh, how I envied Charlie Munger!

It's not because he lived in good health to almost 100, although I think that would be great. Nor is it due to his billions in wealth, even though I too daydream about such riches.

No, the reason I envy Charlie Munger is that, as intelligent as he was, he worked with an equally smart business partner. Charlie described handling his disagreements with Warren Buffett by simply reminding him, "I'm right and you're smart."

What a wonderful phrase. A smart person knows they're right and knows why. When they're dealing with other smart people, they can count on those people to eventually get the point.

I'm smart... and I'm extremely grateful for it

It's become taboo to discuss intelligence across societies. I understand why and while I find the taboo counterproductive, that's another topic. I'll limit myself to direct observation and first-hand experience.

Tested by educators in grade school and again 15 years later before heading to graduate school, my IQ appears to be in the top 1%. This is nothing I can take credit for, just the vagaries of nature. Not taking moral credit doesn't make a high IQ illusory, though.

Being in the top 1% of intellectual ability makes one 25 times more likely to earn a doctorate-level degree than the general population. This is where you find many successful doctors, lawyers, and business executives.

Not surprisingly, one's earning power is linked to IQ as well. I've no doubt being smart put me in a position to earn well. I have a JD and an MBA, and I worked as a lawyer in an executive role at a public company for many years.

A while back, I asked readers what their preference would be if they could choose between intelligence, attractiveness, and wealth. It was one of my most-commented articles and those comments were revealing.

I'm tempted to say smart readers chose the intelligent answer (intelligence), while ugly, stupid people chose one of the other options. But that would be both incorrect and unkind—the sort of thing some writers do for cheap laughs.

Readers' answers were nuanced and thoughtful and I saw valid arguments made for each of the three choices. At the same time, while I understand what led readers to choose beauty or wealth, I could see those choices were much more likely driven by emotion, not cool rationality.

That is the key to the quirk that's made me an annoying debate partner.

I am low on empathy ... and I don't care how that makes you feel

I am not some psychopath completely lacking in empathy. Nor am I a sociopath, who has some understanding of what others feel but chooses to ignore it.

Too bad, or I could have leveraged my intelligence to become CEO of my company. It's also clear to me I could have had a fine criminal career had I further lacked morals and a value system.

No, thankfully I have feelings, and I am aware that others have feelings. I rarely consider others' feelings intuitively, however, or without consciously reminding myself to do so.

Unlike high intelligence, I find having low empathy decidedly less advantageous. I hurt people's feelings by accident, I'm needlessly callous, and I am slow to pick up on social cues obvious to others.

Amidst these negatives, I've identified one significant positive: Most people make most decisions on an emotional basis and then rationalize them (if at all) afterward. I consider most situations analytically and dispassionately and only secondarily (if at all) consider the emotional implications.

This, it turns out, is a superpower. At least it's a superpower if one's goal is to avoid being **passionately wrong**. Incidentally, that is the name of the podcast I host with my friend, Randall Surles

Clear seeing is immensely helpful to clear thinking

My education and my career honed my appreciation for this point: Successfully navigating the world requires an accurate perception of it.

From my psychology degree, I learned that people are a mess of emotions and of predictably irrational behavior. From my economics degree, I learned that incentives directly drive behavior, both positive and negative. From my legal degree, I learned the power of dispassionately analyzing facts and applying a system of rules (the law) to those facts.

Entering the business world, I was amazed to see people confused about why events played out the way they did. Couldn't they see the connection between the inputs and the outputs? Didn't they realize that the design of systems not only predicted certain outcomes but virtually guaranteed them?

Apparently not. The reason, I came to understand, is that many people are led astray by their emotions. They live in the land of wishful thinking. This is what happens when you see what you want to see rather than the world as it actually is.

Wishful thinking applies both positively and negatively, so it'd be more accurate to call it delusional thinking. For example, some perceive slights where they do not exist. Others mistake a systemic advantage for anything but the gift it is.

I seem to dwell in delusional states less often than many people. My hypothesis is that I'm merely lucky to be low on the emotive scale. Together with above-average intelligence, that makes me more inclined to focus on the facts and consider what frame of reference is most useful for analyzing them.

Cogito ergo erras — and it's not your fault

I think, therefore, you're wrong. This sounds arrogant as hell, but now you know why I say it this way.

There are plenty of smart people in the world. A disproportionate number of them are here reading this — after all, who is likely to be attracted to reading and writing like this? I don't fool myself that I'm smarter than many of my readers.

But what is less plentiful are people who can, by disposition like me or via practice like Zen masters, put their emotions to the side and dispassionately look at a situation. That's my default mode.

Thus, when I've written something you find yourself disagreeing with, the chances are good you're wrong. It's your wonderful human emotions that have led you astray.

If you find yourself incredibly annoyed with me right now, I understand. Really, I do.

If you think you can master your emotions enough to put them in the background while debating tough topics, you can take advantage of my method.

Be well.

Chapter Thirty-Six

Thriving In A Low-Trust World

You can, too, by adopting the lawyer's mindset

M any people are angry and confused because the world doesn't make sense.

Our politicians lie and while that's disappointing it's no longer shocking. Worse, each month brings the revelation that another institution has engaged in shading the truth, censorship, or fraud: Universities, scientists, the media, government agencies, corporations, doctors, nonprofits, and the list goes on. Is there no one we can trust?

Among this muddled mess, one group is happily unaffected. You may not have noticed but lawyers are doing just fine. Our worldview is the same as in years past. And our methods of navigating the world work just as well as ever.

Here's what differentiates lawyers and how you can adopt their mindset to maneuver more safely in a post-truth world.

How lawyers see the world — What, not why

One of the best outcomes of a legal education is honing your judgment. By that, I don't mean coming to any moral conclusion about a situation but being able to perceive it accurately.

A person with good judgment can observe a situation objectively, which is the key that unlocks good decision-making. Clear observation starts with simple facts: What happened? Who did what to whom?

Notice I did not include "Why?" as in "Why did this happen?" That's because it's a mistake to ask "Why?" too early. The why is rarely evident up front, which means suggesting a why puts your emotions into the game.

Emotions are like sulfuric acid to clear thinking. Emotions eat away at what's really there and leave you with a burning mix of what you added. Who knows why people did what they did?

A second reason to be wary of the "Why?" is something that every experienced lawyer knows: People lie. They lie blatantly and frequently, whenever it suits them. The most reliable prediction a lawyer can make is that people always lie when they believe it's in their interest to do so.

The sad follow-up is it's almost always in someone's interest to lie. I wish it weren't so, but the legal profession wouldn't exist otherwise.

A more useful question than "Why?" is "So what?" as in "What are the consequences of individuals' actions?

- John punched Fred in the face. So what? Did the police get involved? Did Fred punch John back? Did anyone get it on camera?

- Mary pilfered $1,000 from the petty cash fund. So what? Did she pay it back before anyone found out? Did it come up in our internal audit?

Answering the "So what?" questions requires more than knowing the facts. We also must know the potential consequences of actions. And not hypothetical consequences but practical ones. Can you prove it? If what you say is true, would it matter? What can we do about it?

"I follow you, James, but none of this makes me feel better. People are liars and we can't trust them. We need to look at actions and the consequences of individuals' actions. How does this help me navigate the world?"

How lawyers behave —What can we count on?

Good summary, dear reader, and take heart. Knowing that what people say is untrustworthy means we can give their statements the proper weight: zero. Instead, we look for ways to protect ourselves when it's important. This comes in the form of a handful of contracting principles.

I spent 30 years drafting and negotiating contracts. Millions and millions of them. The primary reason for most contracts is to answer the "So what?" question.

You agreed to buy my car next week for $10,000, which I've told you has 50,000 kilometers on it. A good contract will specify what happens if

- You don't come up with the money in time

- The car has 150,000 kilometers on it

- You decide six months later you don't like it anymore

- And usually a bunch of other things

You can think of contracts this way: Contracts exist to add consequences to otherwise empty statements. "If you lie or fail to keep your promises, there will be consequences, and here's what they are." Contracts turn untrustworthy people (the default) into reliable ones or at a minimum enable us to work together.

Thus, a key rule of thumb is you can count on statements or actions where the person making them is exposed to clear consequences for lying or failure. The corollary is that when there are no consequences for lying or failure, you should not blindly trust the person's statements or actions.

This drastically reduces the scope of what you safely take seriously. That's because people rarely face consequences for mistakes of fact, shading the truth, or outright falsehoods designed to mislead or propagandize.

Just to mention it, the answer is not to surrender trust to people who say things you agree with. They're just as unreliable if they face no consequences for getting it wrong.

Checklist for thriving in a low-trust world

1. Accept that people are untrustworthy and will mislead you when it suits them. It always suits someone.

2. Apply healthy skepticism to claims made when the person faces no consequences for misleading. (Legacy media and publications, social media)

3. Be especially wary of people who want your action or agreement while paying no price for lying. (Politicians, regulators, nonprofits)

4. Seek ways to attach consequences to statements or promises that are important to you. Have explicit "So what" conversations and, yes, sign a contract when the stakes are high.

5. Don't let the quirks of human nature get you down. It's true that skepticism is safer than blind trust, but you needn't become jaded. Forewarned is forearmed and you are now set up for safely making your way.

Be well.

Chapter Thirty-Seven

How To Win an Argument

Effective communication is a joy to behold. Here's a virtuoso display of the method, if we're willing to look past the messenger to the message

W hat do pennies and plastic straws have in common? Some uncommonly good ways to win an argument. If you're open to learning how to use the methods, you will be amazed at how powerful you'll feel.

Important: This post is not about politics. I am using examples provided by President Trump to illustrate the communication and persuasion principles.

Appreciate the skill, if not the practitioner

President Trump has an unusual set of talents, including effective communication. His words are always vivid, emotional, and tangible. They are correspondingly quite persuasive.

It's not just how he creates pictures in our heads. It's the purpose behind those pictures that make them powerful. Two recent examples illustrate what I mean.*

1. Back to black, er plastic, same thing

In a Truth Social post, Trump wrote this:

I will be signing an Executive Order next week ending the
ridiculous Biden push for Paper Straws, which don't work.
BACK TO PLASTIC!

The first sentence sets the stage by highlighting what we disagree with in disagreeable terms. To begin, "ridiculous Biden push" is so strong, calling on fully three levels of emotional reaction:

- No one likes to feel they are behaving foolishly because it subjects them to ridicule. "Ridiculous" thus has us on high alert.

- Biden was singularly unpopular, having been ousted by his own party in favor of a historically unpopular Vice President. Who wants to be associated with that?

- We hate being told what to do, which is exactly what a push does. If we wanted to do it, we wouldn't need a push.

In three words, Trump primes us to expect something foolish, unpopular, and imposed on us by force. He nails it by then naming the culprit, Plastic Straws.

Did you notice the final three words of the first sentence? Devastating, in light of the setup:

- which don't work.

Don't underestimate the power of those words. They underline the frustration much of the population feels about many government policies. Politicians keep pushing stuff on us that doesn't work.

With this, he's tapped into a deep pool of existing, powerful emotions: Anger, confusion, and resentment.

The final words are where the argument is decisively won. The first sentence would be devastating enough but it's negative and leaves a bitter taste (sort of like a disintegrating paper straw on your lips).

Trump ends with an all-caps declaration BACK TO PLASTIC! that is every bit as emphatic as his raised fist after getting shot at the Butler rally.

The tactic he's using: Reframing the argument, taking away your opponent's advantage

- If the argument is about the environment (clean water, happy turtles, pollution), there's no possible way an appeal to plastic could ever win

- In a beautiful judo move of a few words, Trump reframes the argument into (i) not acting foolishly, (ii) resisting yet another push from a government we don't trust, (iii) acknowledging what works and what doesn't, and (iv) taking back individual freedom

As a student of logic, rhetoric, and persuasion, I say this is effective communication. As a psychologist, lawyer, and manager, I say he's won enough hearts and minds that the old argument is effectively dead. Only zealots and fools will now push for paper. Simply masterful.

2. For want of a penny...

What's the President doing worrying about the cost of a penny? Consider this post of his:

> *For far too long the United States has minted pennies which literally cost us more than 2 cents. This is so wasteful! I have instructed my Secretary of the US Treasury to stop producing new pennies. Let's rip the waste out of our great nations budget, even if it's a penny at a time.*

I'll give you a hint: It's not about the penny. This is about cutting off his opponents' argument at the knees without them even realizing it.

The first two sentences set the scene.

- Note the words "For far too long" (how long has it been?), drawing the reader into the narrative from the first words

- "minted pennies" is a strong, visual image — we can almost see the shiny copper coins dropping into the collection vat at the end of the belt

- When making something costs more than twice what it's worth, "This is so wasteful!" is the immediate, visceral reaction. Of course, he's right.

With that setup, no longer producing new pennies is eminently sensible.

What follows, though, is a real kill shot: "Let's rip the waste out of our great nations budget, even if it's a penny at a time."

- "Rip the waste" is a powerful image. We get the sense that the waste won't go willingly. That we'll have to pry it out of the resisting hands of those who benefit from it. That's exactly right.

- "Our great nations budget" reminds us that it is our country and our money we are fighting for. Personal and patriotic at the same time.

- "Even if it's a penny at a time" is wonderful. We all know how hard it is to save money. Many of us had piggy banks as children, into which we faithfully deposited our coins, seeing our small fortunes grow.

The tactic he's using: Taking the moral high ground, making it impossible for opponents to argue against the principle you're championing

- What clueless, arrogant, cold bastard can stand up and say "It's only $40 billion of fraud and waste. There are better things to focus on?" or "It's only 1% of the budget. Why is this important?"

Trump just claimed the moral high ground. The highest officer in the country just reminded Congress and the bureaucracy that every penny counts. It's the citizens' money and not a penny of it shall be wasted.

That's it. The fight over how much fraud, waste, and abuse is OK for Americans to tolerate is over. We don't want a single penny of it lost to grubby theft and malfeasance.

Effective communication is a superpower

Many people struggle to understand how President Trump continues to bounce back from every setback. His rhetorical skills are off the chart. That's contributed greatly to his resilience.

He communicates emotionally, visually, and viscerally. When used together with persuasion tactics like those I've described here, it's a great way to win arguments.

Be well.

* The sharp-eyed among you will have noticed Trump makes typos in his posts and his grammar is often errant. That's the case for both the posts I discussed today. I admit it offends my publisher's eye. But the mistakes are a red herring and we must not get distracted by them.

Chapter Thirty-Eight

How To Get What You Want

Five common mistakes waylay us, but you can avoid them

Individuals often sabotage their progress toward their stated goals. They act in ways that reduce the odds they'll get what they want. Understanding the common reasons for failure can help us avoid them.

Say young Johan desires to become wealthy. He sees wealthy people spending money on expensive houses, cars, and vacations. Johan does the same, although he is not yet wealthy. While he earns a good salary, he does not save or invest but rather incurs substantial indebtedness.

Johan's mistake is obvious to all observing him: One cannot spend their way to wealth. Why isn't it obvious to Johan himself?

1—3. Basic reasons we fail

Possible reasons for Johan's suboptimal behavior include:

1. He is unaware that his spending will have significant consequences, i.e. preventing him from becoming wealthy (**unaware**, *like a baby*).

2. He is aware his financial habits are relevant but is ignorant of better approaches, i.e. keeping his spending modest, investing his savings, and being patient (**uninformed**, *like a child*).

3. He knows of better approaches but is unwilling to take the necessary

steps to implement them (***unrealistic***, *like a young adult*).

Wishful thinking: The unaware, uninformed, and unrealistic

A great deal of self-defeating behavior takes place in these three domains. It is a consequence of willful ignorance and wishful thinking.

Are some people genuinely unaware that smoking dramatically reduces one's life expectancy and is a direct cause of lung cancer? If so, they are keeping themselves ignorant.

How about people who maintain a balance on their credit cards for more than a short period? Have the usurious rates charged by banks escaped their attention? Do they not see how rapidly their balances grow when they make only the minimum payment?

Knowing one's approach is counterproductive to achieving stated goals does not mean one is aware of better alternatives. Think of everyone who fiddles with their eating habits only to see themselves inexorably gaining weight each year.

We keep ourselves ignorant and uninformed because the truth of how we make progress is harsh: It requires patience, discipline, and control to achieve desired outcomes. One must invest time and effort to attain what one wants.

The new employee who proclaims their desire to become CEO in five years while also expecting to depart at 5:00 p.m. and enjoy their work-free vacations is guilty of wishful thinking.

The only antidote for the consequences of willful ignorance and wishful thinking is being confronted with reality. When one's plans go awry and one's goals are frustrated, some are motivated to find a new approach.

To achieve better outcomes, a person must genuinely desire to improve. Wallowing in any of the first three domains thus represents a lack of motivation.

Because we get better results in helping those who wish to help themselves, let's turn to the final two categories.

4. We cannot progress when we lack clear direction

Assuming Johan is acting in good faith, a fourth potential reason he takes actions that appear inconsistent with his goals is this: He may have ill-defined or unstated goals. (***ill-defined goals***, *the mark of a superficial thinker, a person who takes the headline for the news*)

That is, Johan says he wants to become wealthy. But what does "wealthy" mean to Johan? Financial security? The trappings of success? Being able to attract a suitable life partner?

Dangerous waters: The peril of ill-defined goals

This case is at the heart of much of what appears to be flawed thinking and decision-making.

People do things that are demonstrably inconsistent with their *stated goals*. Their actions become understandable when we examine individuals' unstated goals and motivations, which they may not have consciously acknowledged.

The path to improving outcomes for those of us who genuinely want to improve lies in spending more time understanding our motivation and our desires.

Success comes from probing beyond the first answer because it represents superficial thinking. Rather, look to the underlying motives and ask follow-up questions: And why do I want that? Continue to ask the question as many times as necessary to arrive at the fundamental motivation.

You might recognize this as embarking upon asking the Five Whys to gain a deeper understanding.

Johan has realized that his stated goal of becoming wealthy is inconsistent with his behavior of borrowing to fund a rich lifestyle. So he sits himself down for an honest conversation, starting with this question: What is it I truly want? What is motivating me?

- Perhaps Johan realizes that he is insecure about whether he's good enough for his spouse.

- Or he wonders whether the career path he's chosen is the right one for him or whether he's wasting his life.

- Maybe he is so deeply pessimistic about climate change that he believes humanity is doomed.

- Or for Johan, it's none of that, he just wants to enjoy life now while he's young and he's confident he has time to save in a few years.

The point is twofold: Only Johan knows his true goals (which may be inconsistent with his stated goals), and Johan's actions appear differently when measured against his true goals.

If you don't understand your motivation, your actions appear inconsistent with your goals.

Moreover, when you do clearly define your goals, you are (finally) in a position to improve your chances of getting what you want.

5. Critical thinking and decision-making are hard

There is a fifth case, which describes the rest of us most of the time: A person willing to put in a sincere effort to achieve their goals, but who is inexperienced in the available methods or lacks expertise in their implementation (*the inexperienced non-expert*).

This includes everyone who's tried to lose weight by dieting or employed the services of a financial advisor.

The inexperienced non-expert is at risk of the following stumbles:

- Choosing a suboptimal approach

- Implementing a suitable approach in a flawed manner

- Taking further decisions that undermine or undo their progress

Using Johan again, knowing that savings are important,

- A *suboptimal approach* would be keeping his savings in cash under his mattress or in a checking account

- A *flawed implementation* would be buying individual stocks that his brother-in-law recommends

- And *further decisions* that undermine his progress would be cashing in his early investment gains to buy a Ferrari

While avoiding mistakes does not guarantee successful outcomes, committing mistakes guarantees failure.

Thus, we can get what we want more often by avoiding the mistakes I've outlined here.

Be well.

www.ingramcontent.com/pod-product-compliance
Lightning Source LLC
Chambersburg PA
CBHW060322050426
42449CB00011B/2604